W9-ANC-539

MAKING BEER

MAKING BEER

by William Mares

ILLUSTRATED BY JEFF DANZIGER

REVISED EDITION

Alfred A. Knopf   NEW YORK   1994

95639

THIS IS A BORZOI BOOK
PUBLISHED BY ALFRED A. KNOPF, INC.

Copyright © 1984, 1994 by William Mares

All rights reserved under International and Pan-American Copyright
Conventions. Published in the United States by Alfred A. Knopf, Inc.,
New York, and simultaneously in Canada by Random House of Canada
Limited, Toronto. Distributed by Random House, Inc., New York.

Library of Congress Cataloging-in-Publication Data
Mares, William.
Making beer / by William Mares; illustrated by Jeff Danziger. —
Rev. ed.
p.   cm.
Includes bibliographical references and index.
ISBN 0-679-43237-X
1. Beer.   2. Brewing.   I. Title.
TP577.M337   1994
641.8'73—dc20   93-43381
                          CIP

Manufactured in the United States of America

THE LIBRARY
CHESTNUT HILL ACADEMY
500 W. WILLOW GROVE AVE.
PHILADELPHIA, PA 19118

For my father,
who first told me about home brew,
and my wife, Chris,
who helped improve both my beer
and my prose

Contents

Acknowledgments

Many people helped and encouraged me in writing this book. In particular, I want to thank Tom Ayres, Pat Baker, Geoffrey Durnham, Tom Burns, Fred Eckhardt, John Gallagher, Ken Grossman, Paul Hale, Stuart Harris, Michael Jackson, Juergen Knoeller, Jim Koch, Professor Michael Lewis, Steve Mason, Fritz Maytag, Ray McNeill, Lawrence Miller, Steve Morris, Bill Newman, Greg Noonan, George Ouimet, Bill Owens, Charlie Papazian, George Peppard, Mike Redman, Dee Roberson, Todd Scott, Steve Schellhardt, Jim Schleuter, Carol Stoudt, Ralph Swenson, Mark Taverniti, Tom Walters, and Anne Whyte.

Preface

This book traces the evolution of a hobby, that of brewing my own beer. Over a fifteen-year period, this hobby first tempted, then seduced, then abducted me. (For a few hazy months, I wanted to be a professional brewer.)

I now make fifty to seventy gallons of lagers, ales, and stouts each year. I have been president of the Vermont Home Brewers Association. I have won prizes for my beer. I have helped to bring professional brewing to Vermont. At any one time I have three or four cases and kegs of different brews aging in the basement. Proudly, I foist my beer on guests or bring it to dinner parties instead of flowers or wine. I'm happy to talk about beer on any occasion. Thus, some would say the following definition deftly describes my home brewing: "Hobby—an individual pursuit to which a person is devoted (in the speaker's opinion) out of proportion to its real importance" (*Oxford Universal Dictionary*).

I don't use lightly such words as *tempt* and *seduce*. They are appropriate for one raised under the brooding tutelage of John Calvin to believe that work is sacred, that the idle mind is the devil's playground, and, if I may use a twentieth-century metaphor, that vacations are merely pit stops in the race of life. H. L. Mencken, himself an avid home brewer during Prohibition, once described a Calvinist as a person in whose heart lurks the haunting fear that someone somewhere just *might* be having a good time. Well, drinking beer certainly means having a good time. How to square the moral circle?

Learning to brew well enabled me to have my moral hardtack and eat it, too; early failures exacted enough mortification to raise fears that I was predestined to a brewer's hell. Yet my subsequent success and that of thousands of home and professional brewers have given me hope of eventual salvation in a heaven of hops, malt, water, and yeast. I know it is better to give than to receive, but there is no sin in receiving praise in return for a labor of love.

WILLIAM MARES
Burlington, Vermont

MAKING BEER

A Fateful Glass
of Home Brew

My home brewing really began with a bagpipe lesson.

Knowing of my delight in pipe music, my father bought a used set of pipes in England for my college graduation present. For the next few weeks, I made desultory attempts to learn the fingering and play simple tunes on the chanter. I couldn't get a squeak out of the pipes themselves, though, and I soon gave up.

Not until ten years later, when Chris and I moved to Vermont and hired a piper to play at our wedding, did I feel the urge to try the pipes again. Our house was far enough out in the country so that the pagan wailings were but antiphonal to the dogs' and coyotes' howling, but it was obvious that I needed help. After a few inquiries, I learned of a Scott Hastings (surely a promising name), a museum curator and piper who performed around the state.

At his home in Taftsville, Hastings looked over my pipes, took them under his arm, and tuned them for five minutes. Then he made the room reverberate with primitive, spine-tingling melodies. "These pipes are okay," he said, "but they won't play themselves. Playing the pipes is not like raising corn or bees, you know. You have to work at it every day."

As we prepared to leave, he asked almost in passing, "Would you like to try a home-brewed beer?"

At that, his wife, Elsie, suddenly came into focus. While we had been intent on the music, she had been working at the sink, washing out several dozen brown beer bottles. On a chair nearby sat a green garbage can covered with a piece of cheesecloth. Elsie made four or five five-gallon (two-case) batches of home brew each year, and this was bottling day for the latest batch.

Scott disappeared into the basement and returned with a labelless quart bottle. When he pried off the plain cap, the gentle hiss was barely audible. He poured the contents into three glasses until the last portion turned cloudy. It looked like regular beer with its clear, golden color and white, foamy head. It smelled something like beer, mixed with a tinge of cider. I took a sip. It didn't taste exactly like beer. It was both fuller and sharper than the brands I was used to drinking. It had a strong but pleasant aftertaste, sharp but not bitter, quite pleasant.

My only prior exposure to home brew had been secondhand. Like millions of Americans, my father had made home brew during Prohibition. He told me of an experience which was probably repeated thousands of times during those thirteen years of national hypocrisy. He was living in Akron, Ohio, where he worked as a chemist for Goodyear Tire and Rubber Co. He did his brewing in the bathroom and then stored the beer in a closet of his second-floor apartment.

One hot summer's afternoon, the landlady called him at work to say that his beer was exploding and some of it had already leaked through the floor of his apartment. By the time he got home, most of the bottles had burst, the landlady's couch was soaked, and her mood was dark indeed. If he paid for the repairs and cleaning, and promised not to brew again, he could stay. He complied.

It is hard to grow up in Texas without drinking a lot of beer. On the Gulf Coast, where I lived, humid 90° F. weather was possible nine to ten months of the year. In contrast to Vermont, which has "eleven months of winter and one month of damned poor sledding," Texas has ten months of summer and two months of spent "northers," which bring ducks and a touch of frost. In consequence, I always seemed to be thirsty. For Texans, beer is the liquid complement to seafood, barbecue, fried chicken, and, most of all, Mexican food. Like all my friends, I was no beer connoisseur. My favorites were Bud, Miller, and Busch. I scorned regional beers like Lone Star, Pearl, Jax, and Shiner.

I applied to Harvard in part because of Guinness Stout. When I went east to visit colleges in my senior year, my brother, then at Harvard, took me to Cronin's, a popular saloon off Harvard Square. Amid the smoke, vivacious conversation, tweed jackets, and crossed rowing oars, he treated me to my first creamy, black, bittersweet Guinness. Now, this was the college life for me: study all day and drink Guinness into the night.

In Texas I learned to drink beer; at Harvard I learned to hold and appreciate it. On four of the first six Saturdays of my freshman year, I got drunk. I was not lonely, I was not depressed, but no one in the dorm seemed to know any girls, and our way of having fun was to drink Budweiser quarts from the corner liquor store. We varied the routine once or twice by holding contests to see who could down a twelve-ounce can the fastest. The time I won, I did it in 2.3 seconds by cutting two holes in one side of the can and one hole in the other.

But the prizes and wages of our beer blasts were so much retching and wretchedness that I came to hate Sundays and thus moderated my drinking. In those days, American beer was beer was beer. There might have been some differences between Budweiser, Miller, and Schlitz, but they were lost on me.

As it turned out, I didn't drink as much Guinness as I had expected. For special occasions, perhaps twice a semester, we went to the Wursthaus, another Harvard Square watering hole that specialized in foreign beers. But they were too expensive to be dangerously habit-forming for me.

After college, when I worked in Chicago, Jimmy's Woodlawn Tap became my "local," as the English say. Jimmy's, at the corner of Fifty-fifth Street and Woodlawn Avenue, was the only building to survive a wave of urban renewal that swept through Hyde Park in the 1950s. The dirty one-story building had no sign of distinction except for the name embossed on the window. It had none of the polished oak, etched glass, or Victorian decoration that seem to grace most bars near universities.

In 1965, steins of Schlitz and hamburgers were 35 cents each. Bottled beer was 50 or 60 cents. Jimmy had Guinness, Bass, Tuborg, and Heineken. My favorite was Special Export from G. Heileman in Wisconsin. It had a hoppy yet sweetish quality that set it off from the bland monotony of the national brands, and it offered the taste of imported beer at a domestic price.

Jimmy's provided the solid connection between good company and good beer. Beer was the drink of moderation and stimulating conversation. My friends did not drink beer to get drunk. If they wanted to get smashed, they went for the hard stuff.

My other favorite watering hole in Chicago (until it closed in 1967) was the Sieben Brewery, just off Armitage Avenue. Built in 1865, it was both a *Bierstube* and a beer garden. I spent many summer nights sitting in the garden downing steins of Sieben's lager. Sieben did his best to keep the brewery going, but he suffered from the competition of the majors, and the dissolution of the solid German neighborhood that had supported the brewery for so long. In the 1960s, that was enough to kill off dozens of breweries like Sieben's. There were just too few beer aficionados who understood that the major brands offered nothing better than Sieben's except flashier advertising.

I discovered the enormous variety and complexity of beer on travels abroad. As a member of the Harvard Glee Club, I toured the Far East, and after concerts I savored such marvels as Kirin, Asahi, Sapporo, San Miguel, Singha, and Golden Eagle. During a half-year I spent studying in Germany, I drank my fill of Spaten Bräu, genuine Löwenbräu, Hacker Bräu, and seemingly dozens of local beers across Bavaria, Swabia, and the Palatinate.

Later, my work as a journalist took me to Europe and Africa. Our visit to Scott Hastings came a few months after a six-week trip to Ghana, where Chris and I consumed gallons of Club, Star, and locally made Guinness, all full-bodied and refreshing. Each time I returned to the United States, I was more disappointed with the beers offered by our big brewers. I was struck by the blandness, the icy temperature, and the hard-edged fizziness of them all.

I saw that emulating Elsie Hastings would give me a chance to avoid the big brewers. I would create my own beer at a reasonable cost and brew whatever variety I could imagine. Home brewing fit in well with the other strains of self-sufficiency our friends were then practicing in Vermont: sheep raising, beekeeping, vegetable gardening, and the like. That brewing was technically illegal only added to its appeal.

It was several months before I could assemble the necessary equipment from local hardware stores. I bought a ten-gallon green plastic garbage can, a capper, and a gross of caps. At a grocery store, I picked up a can of Blue Ribbon Hopped Malt Extract, five pounds of sugar, several packets of Fleischmann's baker's yeast, and some cheesecloth.

My father gave me a recipe which said to boil a gallon of water, pour in the malt syrup and sugar, boil ten to fifteen minutes, and then add four gallons of tap water to cool the brew to 80° F. Then I was to sprinkle in the yeast. I used a cross-country ski thermometer to measure that final temperature. To keep the flies out of the garbage can as the brew fermented, I draped two thicknesses of cheesecloth over the top and tied it securely. This still permitted me to watch the fermentation's progress. My father had said nothing about cleaning the bottles, so I just washed them out with soapy water, rinsed them, and let them stand.

Faithfully I followed his instructions. However, he hadn't told me that malt syrup has the consistency of 90-weight engine oil. Which meant that as I brought the liquid back to a boil, some of the undissolved syrup stuck to the bottom of the pot and burned. Undeterred, I pressed on. I assumed that since the yeast was to be added at 80° F., the ambient temperature should remain close to that, so I kept the can in front of a window where it was 75° F. during the day.

After about eight hours, a thin film had formed on the surface. The next day, the froth was about an inch deep and looked like dirty shaving cream. It did smell something like beer, though heavy on the carbon dioxide. My father said to let it perk until the head dropped and most of the bubbles disappeared, which should take four or five days.

The head eventually rose to a height of two inches, and then, as he predicted, it subsided. Or rather, collapsed. In one day it fell and disappeared. Since I could still see tiny bubbles rising to the surface, I decided to let the mixture ferment for two more days. After that, no further bubbles were evident. In their place, there appeared miniature lily pads of white moldy material about half an inch across. These were completely unexpected and didn't appear to belong in the beer, so I took a kitchen sieve and skimmed off as many as I could.

After a week, I decided it was bottling time. I carefully spooned a teaspoon of sugar into each bottle to give the beer the necessary carbonation. Then I took a length of plastic hose, held one end in the brew and put my finger over the other end. I sucked out some of the beer to create a gravity feed. It tasted a bit sharp, but not rancid. I assumed that the sugar in the bottles would even out the taste.

I managed to fill fifty bottles and only spilled a quart or so on the floor. I capped the bottles, put them in two cases, and grandly marked the boxes HOME BREW. I carried the cases to the basement and stored them in the coolest corner.

That seemed simple enough.

About a week later, we were having breakfast when Chris asked me if I had heard a jet break the sound barrier during the night. I hadn't.

I didn't miss the second salvo.

As I was washing the dishes, there came a loud *crumpp!* from the basement, followed by the soft tinkling of glass. We didn't need some fancy problem-analysis to understand what was happening: the beer was exploding. The problem now was damage control. Should we leave the bottles there to commit suicide in peace if not quiet? They were next to the washing machine and we'd have to do a laundry sometime during the next week. Should I go down there now and cover the cases with planks of wood? That would mean that eventually all five gallons of beer would end up on the floor and shards of glass would be everywhere.

I decided I had to get the beer outside. So I bundled up in a heavy winter parka and put on Chris's ski goggles and a plastic helmet. Thick mittens and hiking boots completed my armor. While I was dressing, another bottle blew. I found a piece of half-inch plywood about the dimensions of a beer case. With this shield, I sallied down into the basement. The air was thick with the sweetish smell of spilt beer. I sneaked around an oil tank and quickly placed my shield on top of the first case. Gently, I wiggled my fingers under it and made my way upstairs. Only then did I realize I had no protection under my chin. Another explosion might send a cap flying up through the wood to penetrate my lower jaw. Too late for such worries now.

I carried the case out to the barn and put it down in a stall. Mission half accomplished. I was sweating like a pig as I went back for the second case.

Once both cases were safely transported, I felt I just had to try one of those beers. I took an opener back to the barn. Squatting to one side, I raised the lid on a case and extracted a bottle. With its top pointed away from me, I slowly pulled off the cap. With a great hiss, white foam spewed out of the bottle. As this pocket volcano gushed forth, I took the first and last sip of my maiden batch of home brew. It tasted like liquid, carbonated, sweetish, overyeasty bread dough.

REAL
BEER

Back in the house, I stripped off my soaking armor. Whoever said you can't build up a thirst by 9:00 a.m. was wrong. I pulled out a Piels, popped the top with sudden respect for professional brewers, and sat down to watch the sun burn off the early-morning fog. Even as I drew my first deep swallow, another bottle exploded down in the barn.

For the next two weeks, the beer continued to lay down harassing fire, lobbing scornful shells into my enthusiasm. Perhaps, I mused, I should stick to bagpipes and bees. The former required only practice, and the stings of the latter seemed an acceptable price to pay for the sweetness of the honey.

Not an auspicious beginning for a successful home brewer.

A Quick History
of Home Brewing

In the beginning, all brew was home brew. The exact origins of beer are unclear, but the earliest records we have of fermented beverages come from the Tigris-Euphrates valley eight thousand years before Christ was born.

No one knows when the first Sumerian peasant happened upon the idea of soaking hard barley kernels in water to soften them for eating. Similarly, no one can tell when the next peasant in that apostolic succession of home brewers deliberately or inadvertently left some of those soaked grains to dry, chewed on them, and discovered a delightful nutty and slightly sweet flavor. And, finally, it is not clear when the next peasant ground those grains for bread and found that when soaked in water for several days the bread magically transformed the water into something not only drinkable but transporting.

Cuneiform records document brewing in Mesopotamia by 6000 B.C. using a variety of barleys and wheats. In time, about 40 percent of the Sumerian barley crop was devoted to beer production, and wages and salaries were often paid partly in beer.

The priesthood soon realized that people were reaching an altered state of consciousness by drinking beer, so they made haste to sanctify the potion and give it its own goddess, Ninkasi, "the lady who fills the mouth." At the same time, commercial breweries sprang up to slake the thirst of those who could not brew their own.

In his book *The Sumerians*, Samuel N. Kramer writes of Ninkasi: "Although she was a goddess, born in sparkling-fresh water," it was beer that was her first love. She is described in a hymn of glorification addressed to her by one of the devotees of the Inanna cult as the brewer of the gods who "bakes with lofty shovel the sprouted barley; who mixes the happir-malt with sweet aromatics; who bakes the happir-malt in the lofty bin; and who pours the fragrant beer in the lahtan-vessel which is like the Tigris and Euphrates joined."

In the year 2500 B.C., one cuneiform text contained a long list of different words for beer, including dark beer, whitish kuran-beer, reddish beer, excellent beer, beer (mixed) of two parts, beer from the "Nether-World," beer with a head, beer which has been diluted, beer which has been clarified, beer for the sacrifice and beer for the main (divine) repast.

Meanwhile, the art of brewing was also developing in Egypt. There beer was looked upon as a gift of the god Osiris and was an integral part of festivals and ceremonies. In Egypt, beermaking grew directly out of breadmaking. A dough of sprouted, ground grains was partly baked, then torn apart and soaked in water for a day or two, during which time (we now know) fermentation by wild yeasts occurred. The "liquor" was strained off and the beer was ready to drink. Of course, no one knew what yeast was or how it acted on the grain sugars; but in time, brewers realized that when some of the lees of previous batches were added to a new one, the fermentation went faster.

These ancient brewers were not content with the same brew week in and week out. They experimented constantly with different flavors, spices, such as ginger and juniper, and herbs to vary the taste. With the priesthood involved, these "experiments" had strong religious and magical overtones. Beer became the national drink of Egypt. To give a party was to "arrange a house of beer."

Early brewers doubtless had plenty of failures, given the unscientific nature of the process. The Egyptians passed their brewing knowledge on to the Greeks, who in turn carried the brews to the Romans, although both those northern Mediterranean peoples preferred wine.

Meanwhile, the tribes roaming northern Europe were settling down long enough to learn to make beer using native grains, honey, and, later, barley. As early as 2000 B.C. the "beaker people" were producing and selling beer. Early Danes brewed a cross between wine and beer with barley, cranberries, and bog myrtle. The Roman historian Tacitus wrote of Germans who drank a barley-wheat beer spiced with ginger, anise, or juniper.

In medieval England most large households had their own brewing operations. The beers varied in strength from the equivalent of near beer to strong barley wines. The northern European peasantry generally drank large quantities of low-alcohol beer in the same manner and for the same reason that nineteenth-century New England farmers consumed hard cider—it was safer than the water.

Hops, the viny source of modern beer's pleasant bitterness, was only one of many flavors added to beer until the eighth or ninth century A.D. After that, there are records of the continuous use of hops in Bavarian beer. By the end of the fifteenth century, hops had become barley's inseparable partner in most Continental beers.

The introduction of hops into England, however, caused a furor. Lovers of unhopped ale fought a rearguard action against the Dutch hops that had gained a foothold of cultivation in Kent. In fact, Henry VIII banned their importation, but by the end of the sixteenth century the English marriage of hops and barley malt was generally accepted.

Thus the term *ale,* which originally distinguished English beer from hopped Continental beer, came to mean top-fermented (and hopped) English-style brew in contrast to the bottom-fermented (lager) variety. Hopped beer seems to have won the day because of its excellent preservative and sterilizing qualities in addition to its ability to balance the malt. (In the rest of this book, I have adopted the English custom of referring to both beer and ale as "beer." When Shakespeare wrote, "I will make it felony to drink small beer," he meant ale. When I say "ale," I will mean the top-fermented beer.)

The first white settlers in North America brought with them both commercial and home brewing. The Jamestown colony made a poor beer out of Indian corn. The Pilgrims at Plymouth, according to the diary of one of their members, were in distress because they "could not now take time for further search or consideration, our victuals being much spent, especially Beere."

John Alden, a cooper by trade and caretaker of the *Mayflower*'s beer barrels, decided to settle in the new land with the immigrants when he saw their need for beer.

Beer was a staple of the Puritans' diet, as attested by this passage from the diary of minister Richard Mather in 1635: "And a speciall means of ye healthfulnesse of ye passengers by ye blessing of God wee all conceyved to bee much walking in ye open ayre, and ye comfortable variety of our food; . . . we had no want of good and wholesome beere and bread."

In 1630, the year my mother's ancestors came to America from England, one ship, the *Arbella*, left port carrying three times as much beer as water.

Pastors and public officials praised the benefits of beer because it provided a stout defense against the ravages of "strong waters," a euphemism for Demon Rum.

In 1635, within six years of the establishment of the West India Company colony on Manhattan, its Dutch inhabitants had built their first brewery. English and Dutch brewers and home brewers had to weigh the expense and time of securing ingredients from Europe against the search for local sources of supply. The wealthy continued to import beer from Europe, but anyone living even a few miles from the port cities soon turned to his own devices. Home brewing was not a hobby but a necessity.

The colonists used wild hops when they could find them, or substituted ground ivy and juniper berries. One of the most popular alternatives was essence of red or black spruce, which also worked well as a preventative against scurvy.

> *If barley be wanting to make into malt*
> *We must be content and think it no fault*
> *For we can make liquor to sweeten our lips*
> *Of pumpkins, and parsnips, and walnut-tree chips.*

As Mark E. Lender, a modern writer on American drinking habits, has put it: "One suspects that the beers produced from such recipes were little better than the poetry."

Like their English forebears, early American settlers brewed roughly three classes of beer, according to strength. The weakest and most commonly drunk was called small beer. At the other end of the spectrum was strong beer, so defined by the length of time the malt was soaked in water to convert starches into fermentable sugars. Strong beer, which might have 6 to 7 percent alcohol, was a favorite of the wealthier classes, who could usually afford an in-house brewer. In between was middle beer, or table beer.

All these beers were cloudy, an aesthetic fact traceable to the top-fermenting yeast which had evolved in England. One reason for the popularity of hard cider among the colonial elite was that, in contrast to beers of all strengths, the cider was clear. As beer historian Stanley Baron wrote in *Brewed in America:* "The most characteristic aspect of brewing in the seventeenth century, however, was its chanciness. Brewers understood very little about the technology of their trade, and the chemistry involved was a total blank to them. Even measuring devices, such as the thermometer, the hydrometer . . . and the attemperator . . . did not come into practical use until the second half of the eighteenth century. Everything about their brewing was inaccurate and capricious; they could not explain why one brew came out well and the next poorly. The properties and control of yeast remained unexplored until the researches of Pasteur and Hansen in the 1870's. No wonder we find references to 'the art and *mystery* of brewing.' "

Harvard owned three breweries in succession in the seventeenth and early eighteenth centuries, and beer, or its lack, figured in the dismissal of the college's first president. Under the terms of matriculation, President Nathaniel Eaton and his wife were to provide the students with a weekly ration of bread and beer. According to S. E. Morison, in the bill of particulars brought against Eaton, college authorities alleged, and Eaton's wife admitted, that the promised beer was sometimes "wanting . . . a week or half a week together."

Baron suggests that one of the first recorded recipes for home brewing in North America was written down by George Washington:

To Make Small Beer

Take a large Siffer [Sifter] full of Bran Hops to your Taste. Boil these 3 hours then strain out 30 Gallons into a Cooler put in 3 Gallons Molasses while the Beer is Scalding hot or rather draw the Molasses into the Cooler & St[r]ain the Beer on it while boiling Hot. Let this stand till it is little more than Blood warm then put in a quart of

Yea[s]t if the Weather is very Cold cover it over with a Blank[et] &
let it Work in the Cooler 24 hours then put it into the Cask—leave the
Bung [Stopper] open till it is almost don[e] Working—Bottle it that
day Week it was Brewed.

In his retirement, the polymathic Thomas Jefferson turned to brewing with characteristic thoroughness. Baron quotes his answer to an
inquiry about private brewing from James Madison:

Our brewing for the use of the present year has been some time over.
About the last of Oct. or beginning of Nov. we begin for the ensuing
year, and malt and brew three sixty gallon casks . . . in as much as
you will want a house of Malting, which is quickest made by digging
into the steep side of a hill, so as to need a roof only, and you will
want a hair cloth also of the size of your loft to lay the grain in. This
can only be had from Philadelphia or New York. . . . I will give you
notice in the fall when we are to commence malting and our malter
and brewer is uncommonly intelligent and capable of giving instruc-
tion if your pupil is as ready at comprehending it.

The differences in technique between home brewing and commercial brewing were not great, even into the nineteenth century. Until Pasteur's isolation of yeast culture, both had to rely upon the careful
extraction and retention of the lees in which rested the yeast from the
previous batch.

By the beginning of the nineteenth century, there were some 132
breweries in the United States, producing 285,000 barrels annually. (In
the same year, a single London brewery, The Anchor, made 205,000
barrels.)

In 1840, a Philadelphia brewer named John Wagner brought some
bottom-fermenting yeast from Germany to his small establishment on
St. John Street. There, in a kettle hung over an open hearth, he brewed
eight barrels of beer, which were subsequently stored (lagered) in the cellar. (*Lagern* in German means "to store.") From these humble beginnings
arose a tidal wave of lager beer, which by 1880 had engulfed the country.

Before 1840, all beers drunk in the United States were top-fermented
ales, porters, and stouts. After 1880, over 90 percent of the beer was

bottom-fermented lager. There were several reasons for the switch. First, the highly carbonated lager was more thirst-quenching in the hotter climate of the United States. Second, it was clearer and its introduction coincided with the invention of cheap, transparent glass in which to serve the beer. Third, the failed German revolution of 1848 sent thousands of discontented emigrants to the New World. Some of them were brewers, and almost all were lager drinkers. Germans set up hundreds of local and regional breweries in the following years. So ubiquitous were these breweries, and so good were their products, that fewer and fewer people bothered to brew their own. One authority on the history of American food, Richard J. Hooker, also suggests that lighter-bodied lagers were more compatible with Americans' relatively high-meat diet.

The need for refrigeration in both the manufacture and storage of lager made it next to impossible for home brewers to match the store-bought or saloon beer. Home brewing became the province of a few cranks and those isolated on the frontier. People who lived scores of miles from the nearest brewery used recipes not unlike this one from the Australian outback, courtesy of Ian McDonald:

4 lbs. white sugar	3 oz. hops
1 tsp. dry baker's yeast	2 gals. water
1 lb. brown sugar	1 tsp. salt
2 lbs. Saunders Malt extract	

Boil 1 gal. of water in enamel bucket, add hops tied in bag and make it sit down and soak. Boil 20 minutes, take bag out. Squeeze out as soon as cool and put back into brew. While bag is cooling, add all other ingredients except yeast. When everything has dissolved, add the other gallon of water. Stick finger in at blood heat, add yeast at this temperature.

Put bucket in warmest place, possibly a cupboard, and cover with a towel to let air in. Don't move around.

Skim off froth and flies. Leave approximately 7 days in warm place, until top clears and sediment drops. Siphon into another container, anything, wash out sediment, and pour back into bucket. Leave another 24 hours to settle again. Siphon again and then bottle one-third full. Top up with clean water.

Soak bottle tops in water beforehand to wet cork for one half hour.
Cap the bottles. Store bottles standing up in a cool place. Start drinking after a fortnight—preferably a month. Must be cold.

Home brewing returned to the United States under duress. On January 16, 1920, Prohibition became law and millions of citizens like my
father became lawbreakers. Offended equally by the law and by bootleg-
gers' prices, would-be brewers had to start from scratch. There were no
recipe books and certainly no home brew supply shops selling ingredients and equipment. Most home brewers had to rely upon the imperfect
and often foggy memories of their own fathers.

Their chief inspiration was Lena, the round and warm-faced woman
who graced the label of the Blue Ribbon malt can manufactured by
Pabst. Fortunately, malt could still be sold because of its use in baking.

When home brewers couldn't find Lena, they resorted to all kinds of
alternatives, such as corn, rice, and wheat. By and large, the result was
powerful, cidery, cloudy, and tolerable only because of the alcohol it contained.

Joseph De Benedetti, part owner of a home brew supply store in
Portland, Oregon, described his Prohibition brewing:

"We would take a carton of malt, three pounds of sugar and a package of Fleischmann's cake yeast. We used stone jars—six gallons for a
five-gallon batch and twelve gallons for a ten-gallon batch. It usually fermented for one week in the crock. Sometimes you'd put light bulbs
around it to force it, but if you had a cool basement and it fermented
slowly, it made a better beer.

"We'd use two and a half pounds of malt. Bring your water to a
rolling boil, put your hops in, and bring it down to a simmer for about
twenty minutes. That would be the best brew. When it cooled down a little bit, you added your yeast and it would foam up in the first day or two.
You could skim that off, but it wasn't necessary. You boiled the whole
batch at once. Lots of people couldn't be bothered to boil: they'd just mix
it up. Then, depending on your patience, it would be about two weeks
before you drank it. Sometimes it was good, most of the time it was terrible. I always had pretty good luck.

"Everybody claimed they made the best beer in town. They would
make it so darn strong—they would double up on the malt, and the sugar

would all ferment out. They would get a high hydrometer reading, but it wouldn't all turn into alcohol because the yeast can only eat so much sugar. You'd have to give it a second shot of yeast. You would have to have the right temperature—sixty to seventy degrees. It was called a warm fermentation."

Beer drinkers came out of Prohibition with both an enormous thirst and a violent distaste for home brew. The commercial breweries were more than happy to welcome them back with a clear, predictable, inoffensive beer that didn't bite. Drinkers were in no mood to talk about the fine points of beer: they wanted to know and see what they were drinking, and they wanted to drink a lot of it.

In 1876, there were over 2,600 brewing companies in the United States. This number had fallen to 1,100 by 1919. Just over 700 breweries reopened at the end of Prohibition, fourteen years later. By 1976, fewer than 40 brewing companies remained. The reduction in numbers was matched by a similar narrowing of beer styles, as brewers formulated beers according to the lowest-common-denominator principle. In a nation bubbling with ethnic diversity, breweries opted for blandness over distinctiveness, inoffensiveness over pleasure, advertising over ingredients, and adjuncts over barley.

In the 1930s, a few regional brewers began to explore national distribution. To ship their beers from Milwaukee or St. Louis cost an extra "premium," which was added to the local distributor's price. Through the wonders of modern marketing, the brewers were able to convince the public that the premium was an indication of goodness, not a noun describing an extra cost. Hence the term *premium* beers. In actual fact, many of the local beers tasted better than the national ones, but they were overshadowed by the so-called premium brands from breweries that were also able to foot the tremendous costs of national advertising.

Another reason for the "lightening" of American beers was the marketing decision during and after World War II to appeal to women, who were thought to prefer a milder taste. The growth of the take-home market, the packaging of beer in cans, and their ready availability in supermarkets also meant that more and more the decision of which beer to buy was being made by women.

In the 1960s, the Peter Hand Brewing Company in Chicago introduced Meister Brau Lite, and the Gablinger Brewery in New York offered a similar low-calorie beer. They sold modestly well, but were hampered by small advertising budgets. It required the resources of a cigarette maker, Philip Morris, to change the face of American beer. In 1972, Philip Morris acquired Meister Brau and its Lite label and then merged it with the already swallowed Miller Brewing Company. Using the weight and sophistication of a massive advertising campaign, Miller moved from seventh to second place among U.S. brewers (behind Anheuser-Busch) and from 5 million barrels to 31 million barrels in sales. Their slogan became "All you ever wanted in a beer. And less." It was a stunning marketing success, one which Budweiser did not take seriously until Miller Lite had already captured over 40 percent of the low-calorie market. By 1992, low-cal beers accounted for over 30 percent of total American beer sales.

Not everyone welcomed or accepted the homogenization of beer. Students, servicemen, and others who had tasted good beers abroad came home to the sameness of most American brews. The health-consciousness and do-it-yourself movements merged to spawn a breed of people who cared more about what they ate and drank and had the time to prepare that better fare. Some of them were incensed that beer and wine remained the only major food products exempt from federal ingredients-listing requirements. Finally, there were tens of thousands of people who still, quietly, made their own beer in the old-fashioned Prohibition manner, despite home brewing's assumed illegality.

When Prohibition ended, the government specifically legalized the home manufacture and consumption of wine, up to two hundred gallons per two-person household, but it said nothing about beer. For the next forty years, therefore, the public assumed that home brewing was still illegal, although there were no known cases of prosecution for it. Wine supply stores and a number of mail-order seed catalogues began to offer some home brew supplies in the late 1960s and early '70s.

Some of the more enterprising and intrepid winemaking supply stores began to import English malt syrups and extracts such as John Bull, Edme, and Munton & Fison for making beer. The English malting companies, having saturated their domestic markets, looked to the Americans for additional sales. They provided recipes for English ales, stouts, and porters, as well as lagers. Most home brewers were primarily interested in making something that in any case would be clearly different from American beers.

In 1977–1978, an amalgam of California home brewers, led by writer Lee Coe and members of such clubs as the Redwood Lagers, the Maltose Falcons, and the San Andreas Malts, persuaded Senator Alan Cranston to sponsor a bill giving home brewing the same legal status as winemaking. The bill was passed by both houses of Congress and signed by President Carter in 1979.

The key provision of the bill read:

Beer For Personal or Family Use—Subject to regulation prescribed by the Secretary of the Treasury, any adult may, without payment of tax, produce beer for personal or family use and not for sale. The aggregate amount of beer exempt from tax under this subsection with respect to any household shall not exceed—(1) 200 gallons per calendar year if there are 2 or more adults in such household or (2) 100 gallons per calendar year if there is only 1 adult in such household.

Another ingredient in this beer revolution was the rising demand for imported beers. For years, Heineken led the imports, controlling as much as 40 percent of the market (as it still did in 1981). But millions of Americans were now traveling abroad and bringing home pleasant memories of dozens of other brands, including San Miguel from the Philippines, Dos Equis from Mexico, and Fischer's from France. Imported beer sales rose over 1,000 percent during the 1970s and '80s. Still, that amounted at most to 5 percent of the total U.S. beer consumption. In northern Vermont, Molson, Moosehead, and LaBatt's became so popular that many people didn't think of them as imports.

The American beer industry was in turmoil over style, taste, and concentration. It was bisected by seemingly conflicting trends: one group of consumers appeared to want blander, weaker, less distinctive beers—the low-calorie offerings. But another segment demanded heavier, more flavorful, fuller-bodied beers, which were now being marketed as "super-premiums," and the imports. Squeezed in the middle were the regular beers and the smaller regional breweries.

As the major brewers fought each other for a larger market share, they played corporate "Pac Man," devouring one brewery after another until it appeared as if the end of the 1980s would see what Russell Cleary, president of G. Heileman & Co., called a "duopoly" of Anheuser-Busch and Miller.

And where were the home brewers in all this? "Without measurable impact," according to a spokesman for the U.S. Brewers Association.

From Mother Earth to the Heartland and Back

I couldn't give up brewing after one try. If my bagpiping could improve, so could my beermaking. What's more, I had grandly told many friends that my beer would be better than anything they had ever tasted before. It was a way to set myself apart from the talents of fly-fishermen, carpenters, poets, and stonemasons. To quit after one attempt would be mortifying, although I was beginning to realize that brewing was not as easy as I had anticipated.

My father's advice, when he heard of my explosive failure, was to add less sugar. He pointed out that fermentation has two by-products—alcohol and carbon dioxide. The bottles probably blew up because I hadn't completed the fermentation and there was no place for the CO_2 to go.

This time I wrote down every step in my procedure, including the fact that I used two-thirds the previous amount of sugar. I also made one small methodological advance: instead of spooning out one teaspoon of sugar into each bottle, I dissolved the whole amount (about a cup) in hot water and then added the solution to the five gallons of brew just before bottling.

When this batch was bottled, I took it directly to the barn and for the next two weeks checked the cases daily. No explosions, so that was progress. I waited another week before trying some. Wearing my goggles, but not the overcoat, I retrieved one bottle. To reduce the chances

of a gusher, I put it in the freezer for a couple of hours. Then I took it out-side and opened it ever so slowly. A quiet, subtle *shissss* gave me hope, but the first sip dashed all expectation in a puckering bouquet of vinegar. I fetched another bottle. Same result. "Well, there's plenty of vinegar for pickles," Chris said cheerfully. I was not amused. One by one I opened each bottle and sniffed it, hoping to find an exception. No such luck.

It was obvious that in some way this batch had become contaminat-ed. At the town library I looked in vain for home brewing books that might tell me what to do. Nothing. In the *Encyclopaedia Britannica,* the seven pages on brewing contained an elaborate history and description of commercial brewing technology, but nothing about home brew.

For the next batch, I cleaned the garbage can with a chlorine bleach solution, then scrubbed it with baking soda solution instead of soap and water, and topped out with a clean water rinse just before brewing. I also used the garbage can cover instead of cheesecloth, reasoning that, the more airtight I kept the fermenter, the less chance there'd be for contam-inating critters to get in and spoil my beer.

At times I felt as scientific as Lister, Jenner, or Pasteur; at other moments, like a bumbling alchemist. I had told my friends I was brew-ing my own beer, but whenever they asked for a sample, I said I had none left. I didn't reveal that I had thrown out both batches.

This third batch was my make-or-break effort. If it turned sour again, I would go back to my bees. I let it age for a full month. Then, one day, after helping a neighboring farmer hay his fields, I was drenched in sweat and grime. What a fine opportunity to try the brew, I thought. I put two bottles in the freezer and sat down on the stoop with the farmer to talk about the coming deer season.

After ten minutes I retrieved the bottles and casually, if carefully, pried off the caps. There was an inviting hiss. I told him that this was my first "real" effort, neglecting to mention that the others had been total failures. The brew looked clear and it had good foam. It smelled a bit yeasty but, wonder of wonders, it tasted like beer—malty, bitter, and refreshing.

In retrospect, it was probably a typically cidery Blue Ribbon home brew. But I thought it was darned good. And so did my neighbor, at least that's what he said. It reminds me now of our first maple syrup, when we ignorantly boiled the sap down to industrial-grade darkness, or the first honey from our hives, laced with bits of bee bodies. The beer would win no prizes, but it was drinkable and it was ours. The emotional investment blotted out a host of faults.

The farmer finished the whole bottle, sediment and all. I drank another bottle. It wasn't exactly smooth, but the flavor was strong and, I thought, very European.

During the next few days, I found numerous opportunities to tell friends about my brewing success. In fact, I was about as shy and retiring as a new father. A couple of weeks later, a writer/farmer friend, Nat Tripp, invited us for dinner and suggested, "Since your beer is so good, why not bring some?"

On the night of the party, I chilled a six-pack in the freezer and then wrapped the bottles in an old blanket for the drive over the dirt roads, so we wouldn't get hurt if any exploded.

While the other guests helped themselves to gin and tonics or Budweisers, I opened a couple of my bottles. I poured out several glasses and carried them to the guests. The head disappeared in the first twenty seconds, but Nat sniffed appreciatively. "Ah, there's no smell quite like that of home brew!"

Looking like royal servants tasting for poison, two other guests sipped the beer. They paused, their faces stiff masks of politeness. "A little young?" one queried between clenched teeth. "Five weeks," I replied. "Perhaps it needs to age a bit more." The other guinea pig said, "It's okay for home brew," and set the glass down, never to touch it again. One lawyer friend didn't mince words: "You don't mean you prefer this to Bud?"

I laughed, but inside I was hurt. I felt as if I had just helped an elderly lady across the street and instead of thanking me she had kicked me in the shins. I drank the rest of the six-pack myself.

A week or so later, a letter arrived from Tripp. Inside was an article about home brewing from that back-to-the-land missal, *Mother Earth News.*

The article began with a rather mystifying editor's note:

The Justice Department of the Federal Government long ago announced that it would pursue a hands-off policy on any beer made for home consumption and not for sale. In recent years, however, the Alcohol and Tobacco Tax Division of the Treasury Department has informally attempted to enforce commercial laws on home brewers and, thereby, discourage another time-honored, down home, do-it-yourself activity.

Lawyers say the Feds' argument would never hold up in court. Nevertheless, we do not encourage anyone to brew any beer until he is thoroughly satisfied that such activities are completely within the law and that he has complied with all applicable federal, state and local regulations.

Perhaps the editors wanted to cover their rears so the ATF (Alcohol, Tobacco, and Firearms) agents would not swoop down on their office and rummage through their stash of goat's milk and granola bars.

The article itself was decidedly schizophrenic. It delighted in accounts of "friends who experimented with ginger, cracked corn or corn meal. The results were no longer beer but a high octaine [sic] mixture similar to mead. Some of these formulas laid out respectable beer drinkers like they were school boys." On the other hand, it did stress the danger of bottling too early and recommended recording recipes so the brewer could repeat the ones he liked and, presumably, avoid repeating the failures.

Mother Earth News tossed me into the first of several briar patches of conflicting or just plain lousy advice and information. Had I a conspiratorial turn of mind, I might have believed that the writers of this and other articles were ATF agents spreading black propaganda or disinformation about the home brewing craft as a means of suppressing it.

To its credit, the article did help me produce drinkable beer about one time out of three. I poked along for a couple of years, making about four batches a year, knowing I could drink the results even if my friends opted for Bud and Molson. Many bottles did taste like overfermented cider. When I noticed that guests tended to leave glasses of the beer untouched under chairs or to nourish the ferns with it, I realized that home brew was not for everyone. Brewing on this level was like a low-grade addiction: I couldn't give it up, but it didn't incapacitate me.

In the mid-1970s, I worked for a newspaper across the Connecticut River in New Hampshire. It was at least a forty-five-minute drive home even on clear nights, and in snow it could take twice that long. I confess that I often drank a sixteen-ounce bottle of home brew on that drive most nights—one to get to the river and one to get home from there. On particularly hot and thirsty summer evenings, I would buy one of those huge twenty-six-ounce cans of Foster's lager, which look more like oil cans than containers to hold beer.

I learned that there were more sophisticated ways to brew when I found an elementary text in a secondhand bookstore in Boston. *Home Brewing Without Failures,* by H. E. Bravery, made interesting reading but was almost useless for any practical brewing. He called for ingredients unobtainable in the U.S., like Demerara sugar and roasted malt. What's more, his recipes required such procedures as immersing a heater in the grain and water for eight hours. I just wanted to make beer, not start a brewery.

The New Hampshire newspaper fell victim to the recession, and Chris and I moved so I could take a job in Grand Rapids, Michigan. Grand Rapids remains in my memory a city dominated by the automobile, churches, and beer. We rented half a house across from a Dutch Reformed church that held services in English at 10:00 a.m. and in Dutch at 2:00 p.m. Our landlord next door warned us that people in Grand Rapids took the Sabbath seriously and asked us not to wash the car or mow the grass on Sunday. In his own family, even the "work" of cooking was not done on Sunday.

For most of that year, I was a night police reporter covering fires, highway fatalities, murders, and lesser crimes. When I went out to drink beer with my fellow reporters, I found myself more conscious of their drinking habits. Most of them consumed great quantities of "Fire-Brewed Bohemian Style" Stroh's. On all occasions, drinking was characterized by a race to fill the table with empty bottles and tell stories of past drinking bouts and hangovers. The bars seemed full of boisterous yet lonely people. To them beer was simply a means for getting drunk; not a drink to be savored for its taste. I didn't think of myself as some effete Eastern drinker merely recoiling from the butter-and-eggs boozers of the Midwest. I was sure it was the memory of my struggles to make decent home brew which alienated me from these drinking bouts.

Returning one evening from covering some mayhem, I drove by a store called the Village Wine Cellar, which sold home wine- and beer-making supplies. I went back the following day, and from the moment I entered that room, redolent with the odors of hops, malt, and wine concentrates, my life and beer were never the same.

The proprietor, with the preoccupied air of an academic researcher, introduced himself as Tallmadge Nichols and invited me to browse. One side of the room was devoted to winemaking supplies—grape-crushing tubs, racking equipment, corking devices, cans of fruit concentrate, etc., all displayed under posters of sunny California or France.

It was the other side that caught my fancy: half a store containing home brewing supplies. Back and forth, like a shopper without a list, my eyes roamed from cans of Munton & Fison malt syrup standing like Grenadier Guards, to bags of green- and brown-leaved hops. One shelf held boxes of top-fermenting and bottom-fermenting yeasts. There were bags of hops powders and pellets with exotic names like Bullion, Cascade, and Hallertau. There were small vials of white powders labeled sodium metabisulphite, gypsum, brewing salts, and packets of a brown material that looked like seaweed (and was) but went under the name of Irish Moss. On the floor were large white plastic tubs with tight fitting lids.

"That's food-grade plastic," Nichols said, breaking into my mental comparison with the green garbage can I used. "Sometimes you can get off-flavors from the other kinds of plastic." Coils of clear plastic hose lay nearby like a whaler's rope. There was a group of glass carboys such as I used to see in office water coolers. Atop each one was a Rube Goldberg device of stiff clear plastic. Near the cash register stood a revolving book rack with manuals and pamphlets about wine- and beermaking.

"I'm in your hands," I told Nichols. "What do I need to make good home brew?"

Nichols led me into the back room. From a refrigerator he drew out a plain brown bottle with a silver cap, and from a shelf he retrieved a long-stemmed beer glass. After carefully opening the bottle, he poured a golden beer into the glass, apologizing that it was only a month old.

That first sip sounded the death knell for my *Mother Earth News* beer. This brew was smooth, bitter without being sour, sweet without being sugary, and well balanced. "How can I make some of this?" I asked. "Very easily," he replied. "We have a standard recipe which we give out to all first-time brewers, and they seem quite satisfied." He added that he didn't generally offer beer to someone off the street, but I seemed to be genuinely interested and not just looking for a free drink.

Nichols had started the store about ten years earlier and first con-
centrated on winemaking equipment. Home brewing was then limited to
Blue Ribbon malt extracts. Its technical illegality and the power of commercial beer advertising had effectively deterred manufacturers from
offering a variety of home brewing products for the American market.

In the early 1970s, when British malt manufacturers began to ship
their products across the Atlantic, Nichols was one of the first retailers
willing to stock them. Along with the ingredients came books by Eng-
lishmen, such as Dave Line's *Big Book of Brewing,* C. J. J. Berry's *Home
Brewed Beers and Stouts,* and Ken Shales's *Advanced Home Brewing.* The
language and measurements were British and a bit confusing. Then the
maltmakers began to offer home brew kits with all the ingredients for a
batch at a package price. "That changed the market," Nichols observed.
"What's more, they provided much better recipes and advice than had
existed before."

I told Nichols how faulty I thought the *Mother Earth News* recipe
was. Nichols, a man obviously not given to hyperbole, agreed it was
"exceedingly bad."

"Most of my customers are more price-conscious than quality-
conscious. They want it simple and easy and cheap. They don't want to
make a lot of measurements." On the other hand, heavy beer drinkers did
not patronize Nichols's store, because "a man who consumes one or two
six-packs a night would go through a batch of home brew in less than a
week. Such people don't want to spend all their spare time brewing and
bottling. In fact, those who make their own beer probably end up drinking less than when they buy it, because they have put some of themselves
into the brewing."

The few customers who learned their brewing during Prohibition
were convinced that nothing could improve their beer. They scorned the
English malts as expensive and effete.

"Prohibition-style brewers never spend much time or take temperature readings," Nichols went on. "They put the beer in a container and
start drinking it in three days whether it is in the bottle or not. They think
that is the only way to make beer. They come in and want to argue that
their way is the only way. I don't like to argue. Maybe I have converted a
few, but if they've made it the old way, it is not likely they will change.

The commonest converts to home brewing are those who start from scratch, with no previous knowledge or prejudices."

The lager recipe Nichols gave me called for a can of Munton & Fison malt syrup, dextrose or corn sugar, and Hallertau hops pellets, whose aroma he told me was filling the room.

"You will need some more equipment than I presume you own now," he said. "A secondary fermenter, for example. That's what those carboys are for. Beer needs to ferment under completely airless and thus bacteria-free conditions. Good beer needs to be aged. The plastic device on the carboy is a fermentation lock, or bubbler, which allows the carbon dioxide to escape from the beer without admitting any airborne contaminants. You have to keep water in that bubbler," he warned. Several of his customers had neglected this requirement and wondered why their beer spoiled. "And don't boil the darn thing," he added. Another customer, in a fit of sterilizing frenzy, had done that, and the bubbler had melted into strange and unusable contortions.

Nichols's rule of thumb was to leave the beer in the primary plastic bucket for four or five days for the first bloom of fermentation to occur, then transfer it by plastic tube into the clean secondary fermenter, where it remained until the bubbles in the airlock came only every ninety seconds. Depending upon the ambient temperature, the aging could take two to four weeks. At that point, he transferred the five gallons back to the (cleaned) primary, added a cup of dextrose dissolved in hot water, and bottled it in a fashion I was familiar with. He had, however, improved upon my procedure of controlling the flow by pinching the end of the plastic tube with my fingers: he sold plastic twist valves, which reduced the mess and saved about a quart of beer.

I tried my first batch the following Sunday. The directions were simple. I mixed the malt, dextrose, and hops and boiled the lot for forty-five minutes. Then I poured the wort into the primary, freshly cleaned with baking soda and hot water, added enough tap water to make five gallons, and sprinkled the powdered yeast on those untroubled waters.

By the middle of the Dutch services that afternoon, the yeast had begun to work, for there was a telltale layer of tiny bubbles forming on the surface. I carried the forty-five pounds of bucket and liquid to the cool basement and let it perk for the next five days, allowing myself one sniff each day. The surface showed an ugly eruption of gray and brown foam, like Bluto's shaving cream. It smelled inviting, sharp, and fresh, and much hoppier than my Vermont home brew. After five days, the foam had receded and I transferred the brew to the carboy. Like an explorer planting the flag, I attached the fermentation lock and dropped a black plastic garbage bag over the carboy to keep out the light.

I then hauled the carboy back up to the dining room and placed it in a corner. For two weeks, it sat there, a squat black sentry with a gradually less frequent hiccough: *blup, blup, blup*. By the end of the second week, the bubbles had slowed to one every ninety seconds. With Clorox, hot water, and baking soda, I cleaned out two cases of Stroh's bottles. I made up the priming sugar and poured it into the clean primary fermenter, then transferred the beer from the carboy, using a plastic tube. About a quart of yeasty sediment remained on the bottom of the carboy. The bottles I stored in the coolest corner of the basement.

For three weeks, I made impatient moves in their direction. None blew up. One night, after covering a train wreck and a homicide, I felt I really deserved a beer. I stuck one in the freezer, sat down, and waited for fifteen minutes.

When I popped the top, there wasn't much foam, but what a taste!— as good as that which Nichols had served me—smooth, good balance of hops and malt, none of that liquid bread or stiff cidery taste of Prohibition pilsner. I was so pleased that I had another bottle at cellar temperature and went to bed luxuriating in my first real success.

In the following months, I brewed several more batches, varying either the malt or the hops, but not both. Each time the beer tasted different but still good. Along the way, I made my first convert, Roger Conner, an environmental lawyer. Working sixty hours a week and rebuilding his house wasn't enough for Roger. He needed more things to do. Carpentry gave him a thirst, so home brewing was a natural adjunct. I gave him Nichols's recipe and lent him the ingredients. Fortunately, he knew how to follow directions, and his first effort was as good as my fourth.

I had no success in sharing my home brew with my hard-drinking newspaper friends. They were not interested, and I didn't force them. I kept Stroh's and Pabst on hand for their visits and, I confess, a few bottles for myself. I knew that they and the imports were still better than my beer.

After a year in Grand Rapids, I found a newspaper job back in Vermont. By the time we left, I was making a fair "house" beer. When we packed the U-Haul for the journey home, the carboy, plastic pail, tubes, and capper were as much a part of our belongings as the dictionary, typewriter, and dog.

The Great Grain Wreck

My first Vermont brewing acolytes were two newspaper reporters and a photographer. We started the evening with two six-packs of the Canadian malt liquor Brador, which one reporter had brought back from a trip to Montreal. By the time we had finished boiling the wort for a Grand Rapids lager, we were pretty rowdy. (The wort is the malt-sugar-laden liquid prior to fermentation; if it has been boiled it is called "bitter" wort, as opposed to sweet.) I lost track of the measurements halfway through the brew, but I didn't think it would matter. The next morning, I realized that in my alcoholic fog I had forgotten to put in the yeast. That batch was eventually drinkable, but it had an off-taste that was no doubt related to my lack of attention.

As I brewed my batches of Nichols's lager every couple of months, my consumption of commercial beer declined steadily, although, like a vegetarian who sneaks hamburgers, I would regress on occasion. For several years, I didn't force my beer on anyone. Twice burned, thrice shy of offending others. Even when a few people asked for it, I was a master of self-deprecation: "This isn't for everyone," I would warn. Or, "Like the moonshiner said, the only thing I guarantee is that you don't go blind."

But gradually the balance shifted in favor of my own brew. Chris would drink three or four bottles a week, and an occasional friend might enjoy a glass. When we brought some to a party, a few guests would try it. I drank at least one bottle a night. This meant that the two-case batches were being consumed at a much faster rate than before, like snow melting on a warm spring day.

I had three options: cut down on my consumption, buy more commercial beer, or make larger amounts of my own. I chose the third alternative.

Two obstacles presented themselves. The first was that Burlington water tasted funny. The municipal water system was antiquated, having remained unchanged for seventy years. The water department was about to present a multimillion-dollar bond issue to the voters, but even if it was approved, repairs would not be completed for four years. To compensate for the failing mechanical and piping system, the city dumped more and more chlorine and other chemicals into the water, until it seemed as if you were brushing your teeth in a public swimming pool.

I needed better water. I started carrying empty gallon milk or cider jugs in the trunk of our car, and whenever we visited friends in the country I filled up with their water. This meant that I rarely used water with the same chemical balance twice, but that inconsistency didn't seem to matter in the long run.

The second obstacle was that, even as I perfected my technique for Grand Rapids lager and adopted it as my steady brew, I felt twinges of boredom. I began to thirst for some ale and stout, and some different-tasting lagers. One day, as I was looking through our bookshelves for something to read, I found the three home brewing booklets I had bought in Grand Rapids but had never opened. I chose Byron Burch's *Guide for the Home Production of Fine Beers*.

Burch's book opened with two recipes for a light-bodied pale ale and a dark beer. They seemed pretty complex and involved. There were "flavoring" hops and "aromatic" hops added at different times. The recipe also called for citric acid, gypsum, noniodized salt, and yeast food.

"If you're a beginner reading this for the first time," Burch wrote, "you're probably bewildered by now by the mass of unfamiliar terms swarming about your head. Don't panic, though, because explanations are coming up, starting here." He was as good as his word. He wrote clearly and well about plastic fermenters, thermometers, and hydrometers, why and how the last are calibrated. Echoing Nichols, Burch recommended food-grade plastic, not cheap garbage cans or crocks. Along the way, he offered good advice, suggesting the home brewer should always clean a new primary fermenter with bicarbonate of soda to neutralize any solvents that might be left over from the manufacturing process. He also described the advantages of cheesecloth and secondary fermenters.

In the "Ingredients" section, Burch discussed different kinds of malt (pale malted barley, crystal or caramel malt, black patent malt, Munich malt) and various sugars (dextrose, sucrose, lactose, brown sugar). He devoted three pages to hops, including "flavoring" hops and "aromatic" hops, and explained the difference between leaf hops, hops pellets, and hops extracts. Since Nichols's recipe called for Hallertau hops, I had not looked further, because I was perfectly happy with them at the time, but Burch described hops with evocative names like Pride of Ringwood, Talisman, Brewer's Gold, Cluster, and Northern Brewer. He classified them objectively according to their relative bitterness, and subjectively according to their aroma.

I also learned more about yeast, that marvelous, mysterious, single-celled creature that is the *sine qua non* of baking and brewing. I came to understand the distinction between the top-fermenting strain used for ales and the bottom-fermenting variety common to lagers.

Baker's yeast does work for beer, but it has several major drawbacks, Burch said. It reproduces best at higher temperatures, where the threat of infection is much greater; it doesn't settle well, and thus home brew made with it is always cloudy. Finally, it was developed to create the maximum amount of carbon dioxide to make bread rise. Now I understand why my early beers tasted so yeasty.

Under "Optional Equipment," Burch listed items like a bottle-washer sprayer that could be attached to a kitchen faucet, hose clamps to aid in bottling, and an office scale for measuring small amounts of hops. Other items were familiar—good, solid, returnable green or dark-brown bottles and a strong capper. I felt like a pioneer, long in the woods, who happens upon a general store.

When I finished the book, I thought ruefully how helpful it would have been five years earlier, when I'd started brewing. But it hadn't been available then. Fortunately, I didn't have to look far to find some of the supplies he wrote about. Garden Way Living Center, a division of the Garden Way companies devoted to self-sufficient living, had several shelves of home wine- and beermaking paraphernalia.

However, for all the richness of its selection, the store did not carry any of the flavoring hops varieties Burch recommended for his light-bodied pale ale. All it offered was Fuggles, Cascades (which Burch recommended for aromatic hops), and my old workhorse, Hallertau. On the spot I formulated a rule of thumb for the home brewer: Be flexible. Never be afraid to substitute and create your own recipes, because no home brew store is ever likely to carry all the exact ingredients required for any but the most elementary of recipes.

The major purchase from Garden Way was my first hydrometer. Burch thought it indispensable. As a "brewer's compass," it allows you to measure the progressive conversion of sugars into alcohol and carbon dioxide. The hydrometer calculates the specific gravity or weight of the liquid. Sugar dissolved in water is denser or heavier than plain water, whereas alcohol is lighter. As the yeast converts sugars, the density of the solution falls and thus the hydrometer will sink lower in the solution. The scale inside the instrument shows the potential alcohol when you start, so you can accurately predict what the final alcoholic content will be.

Burch explained that the higher the ratio of malt sugars to corn sugars, the higher the final gravity will be, because malt sugars are not refined enough to convert completely. Some of their solids always remain in solution and keep the final gravity above 1000. Burch made this explanation clear and concise, but another home brew book quite blithely ordered the brewer to bottle only when gravity reached zero. Once a friend of mine left a batch in the secondary for three months, waiting for it to reach that impossible figure.

The best ingredients and recipes are only as good as the containers in which the brewing occurs. Cleanliness here is as close to goodness as it is to godliness. Thanks again to Burch, I learned about the marvels of bleach and sodium metabisulphite. Chlorine bleach is an excellent sterilizer and cleanser when used carefully and rinsed out thoroughly. If bleach is followed by a rinse of sodium metabisulphite, the vessels and bottles will have no residual film or aftertaste and should be clean enough to thwart all infection. Conversely, I finally understood that soap and detergents are anathema to good beer, because of the film they leave behind. That is why many bars don't use soap on their beer glasses—soap and detergent kill the head. The head may be extraneous to the taste, but beer without a head looks more like ginger ale than beer.

When I turned to the other brewing books, I was glad I had read Burch first. They were inferior volumes of oversimplification and outright error. One called itself a "complete" guide to home brewing but turned out to be nothing more than a marketing device for the author's products. It asserted, for example, that "Years of experimenting with the various yeast strains has established that the ———— brand [the brand he happened to sell] is the best yeast for all beers, including stout."

In the next year, I made six or eight batches from Burch's book: pale ales, brown ales, lagers, and a "steam beer." I experimented with adding small amounts of salt, gypsum, citric acid, and gelatin to clear the beer. I really couldn't tell if these ingredients helped the taste, but they made me feel more professional.

Overall, Burch's beers were noticeably better than my Grand Rapids lager, although the difference between them was not as great as between Grand Rapids and the original Blue Ribbon brew. I loved to experiment with different ratios of malt to hops in the hope I could approximate some of the great beers of the world, like Guinness or Spaten Bräu. That I didn't come close didn't matter.

Home brew began to find a niche as a liquid "thank you." It became an offering of something more personal than money or words. I have given beer to the town employee who graded our dirt road in St. Johnsbury. I have used it to thank the plumber for fixing our furnace on a wild wintry night. The manager of the restaurant supply store where I buy brewing equipment earned a bottle for his help in finding a stainless-steel pot. When we burden the garbage man with extra debris, he gets a home brew. The stereo repairman who fixed a receiver free of charge won a six-pack of porter.

Exchanging beer for services probably placed me in the underground economy and, thanks to bartering, I made another convert. Professor Peter Seybolt is a man of many parts—a good tennis player, fly-fisherman, and pig farmer as well as a teacher of Chinese history. In his farming capacity, Peter asked us to trade some of our labor for some of his spiced sausage. I brought a six-pack of home brew to drink as we ground and packed the slippery meat. Then we invited him to help us bottle a batch in return for more home brew. As we bottled, he became so intrigued that he went to Garden Way and bought all the necessary equipment.

My reputation as a home brewer began to spread like the smell of French fries out of a diner's ventilator. This was literally as well as figuratively so, for when I brewed a batch and turned on the exhaust fan above the stove, one could smell the Mares brewery three houses away.

One evening, during a conversation with friends who owned a small construction company, I learned they had registered the name Lake Champlain Monster Brewing Company with the Secretary of State. The name referred to the local version of the much-sought denizen of Loch Ness. That summer there was a flurry of "sightings" of the monster. A minor tourist attraction was born. Although they were not brewers, these friends were hearty beer drinkers who dreamed of a combination saloon and brewery that would dispense Monster Beer to students and tourists. I was intrigued enough by the idea to suggest an intermediate step—put a notice in the paper to solicit interest in a home brewing club. I thought these future commercial brewers ought to have some practical experience.

The organizational meeting of the Vermont Home Brewers Association took place at the construction company's warehouse one warm August evening. Each person was to bring a six-pack or its equivalent of his favorite beer. I was the only one to bring home brew. The others provided the likes of Fischer's, Guinness, Beck's, and Moosehead.

I knew all seven people present except Barton Merle-Smith, late of Boulder, Colorado, and then the owner of Barton's Hot Tubs in Burlington. Barton's ample midsection was covered by a stained T-shirt emblazoned with an emblem of the American Homebrewers Association: a smiling turkey clasping sheaves of barley in one foot and an overflowing bottle of home brew in the other.

It was soon apparent that Barton knew a lot more about home brew than I did. For an hour he regaled us with stories about brewing in Boulder and the American Homebrewers Association. The AHA, we learned, had been founded early in the 1970s by a nuclear-engineering dropout and alternative-school teacher named Charlie Papazian. He began teaching home brewing for a little extra cash and launched the organization out of a spare room in his house. He applied for and received tax-exempt status from the Internal Revenue Service, which made contributions tax-deductible. Here was a philanthropic organization dedicated to spreading the gospel of home brew. Barton passed around copies of the AHA journal, *Zymurgy,* the only magazine I've ever seen that defines its title on the cover. "Zymurgy: dealing with the fermentation process, as in brewing." The motto of the AHA is "Relax. Don't Worry. Have a Homebrew!" When I later sent them $50, I became a Diamond-Studded Platinum Mug Sponsor with a membership card which expired "Never."

Barton's first brew was called Long Distance Lager, because he had made it according to directions from his brother in Boulder during a two-hour telephone call. Like a film dissolve, that story merged into his description of a "beer and steer," where a whole cow was roasted and the guests consumed five or ten kegs of home brew and then jumped naked into a bank of hot tubs.

Zymurgy was full of good information, book reviews, discussions of technique, and accounts of local and national home brewing contests. There were recipes with names like Danger Knows No Favorites Dark Lager, Goat Scrotum Ale, and Whitey's No-Show Ale. Sprinkled through-out its well-illustrated pages were anecdotes and one-liners. Stealing from Fat Freddy of the Fabulous Furry Freak Brothers comics, one wag paraphrased, "Home brew will get you through times of no money bet-ter than money will get you through times of no home brew."

P. T. Davis of Seattle captured the spirit of home brewing when he wrote in the Letters column: "I survived Mt. St. Helens, although not by much—drank too much home brew Saturday night, May 17, and over-slept, thus did not arrive at Spirit Lake in time for my demise. Relax and have a home brew. It saves lives from volcanoes and no doubt from other disasters as well."

Even the club notes brought chuckles for some of the names. Besides the Maltose Falcons and San Andreas Malts, there were the Mile-high Masterspargers, Redwood Lagers, San Gabriel Valley Wort Hogs, and the Christian Ferment League at Princeton Theological Seminary in New Jersey.

Zymurgy introduced me to a whole subculture of home brewers. These were not people who just poured more sugar into the brew to give it a bigger alcohol boost. Nor were they old-line, stalwart home brewers who were satisfied with Blue Ribbon malt. Brewing was part of their lives, just like buying coffee or planting peas in the spring. They formed a collection of serious beermaking cranks, technocrats, and mavericks who still valued the fences of good recipes and directions. They were restless experimenters who enjoyed what one called their "mud-pies-for-adults" activity.

I reported on my eighteen-month campaign to have a home brew contest at the Champlain Valley Exposition, the state's largest fair. The year before, I had tried to interest fair officials in the idea. I argued that home brewing was an ancient and honorable craft, which gave its practitioners as much pride and demanded as much skill as the making of quilts and apple pies. Furthermore, President Jimmy Carter had just signed the bill that permitted the manufacture of up to two hundred gallons of home brew per household. What better way to spread the word than to have a home brew contest? The clinching argument, I thought, was that the home brew law specifically allowed its transportation to public places for the purpose of judgings and tastings.

The fair manager listened politely, but explained that six weeks was not enough time to get directors' approval and insert a new category in the program of prizes. He suggested that I resubmit the proposal the following year.

The week after the club meeting, Barton, who had been elected president, and I put on clean shirts, packed two bottles of home brew in a briefcase, and went to see the manager. He told us he had already recommended that the contest be allowed. The fair board of directors had given its approval, provided it was legal. That meant they wanted to ask the Liquor Control Board, which oversees all distribution of alcohol in the state. I thought we were home free. The fair already had a beer sales tent. We were only proposing that home brew be sipped by four judges. None would be sold, and none would be given away.

Just to be on the safe side, a lawyer friend and I went before the Liquor Control Board's monthly meeting to repeat our request. We were greeted with a few hearty jokes but no decision. The board felt it should submit the question to the state attorney general. All this buck-passing made me nervous, but I still believed that no open-minded person could quash such an innocent activity. After all, the board was in the business of peddling hard liquor to the Vermont public.

Alas, we had not plumbed the depths of caution of that body and of an assistant attorney general who recommended denial on the basis of a Catch-22 statute which said in effect, "Thou shalt not do anything except as provided in this law." Their interpretation was that our contest amounted to free distribution and consumption of beer and was therefore illegal.

Outraged, I went to the county state's attorney and persuaded him to write a letter to fair officials saying that if such a contest were held, he would not prosecute, because he had "more important things to do." The authorities remained unmoved.

(A year later, I saw a member of the Liquor Control Board on the street and asked if we would ever be allowed to have our contest. He lowered his voice, winked, and said, "Just don't ask next time.")

The Burlington *Free Press* tried to mediate editorially, suggesting that we ask for a license to *sell* the beer, the better to comply with the law. "It's just possible that what the Vermont Home Brewers Association could not give away might be all right if they charge a fee." I was intrigued with the idea, but so annoyed at the mixture of narrow interpretation and timidity along the line that I didn't pursue it.

A few days later, I received a call from Steve Morris of the Cram Hill Brewers Association, the only other home brew club in Vermont. I had heard about these ten or fifteen people, most of whom worked at the Vermont Castings stove company in the town of Randolph. They were so well organized that they even had a club song. It purposely didn't have any words, so the members couldn't forget them. Morris had been quoted in *Zymurgy* as saying, "The American beer drinker has less variety available to him than any other beer drinker in the world. Cram Hill Brewers Association tries to promote organically pure, tasty beer and lots of varieties." Having read of our tribulations with the Liquor Control Board, he generously offered, "Let's have the contest at my house. We have an annual eight-mile road race, the West Brookfield Classic, and a sheep roast on Labor Day. We won't make a big deal of it, just invite the people we know. It would be great to add a home brew contest to the celebration."

By the time he hung up, I had agreed to rally all the home brewers I knew and take their entries down to West Brookfield (pop. 50). If brewers wanted to come in person, so much the merrier. We thought that fifteen entries would mean success and twenty-five would make a "happening." Cram Hill members would provide the storage, ice, judging paraphernalia, and prizes. Publicity we would not seek. I was amused at the thought of state police raiding the contest and breaking all our bottles. After a few beers, we would have no trouble "going limp" to passively protest our right to taste, judge, and drink home brew in public. As a precaution, we took along an attorney, ostensibly to watch his son run in the race, but with the secret plan that he would represent us if the police swept in to enforce that ridiculous law.

Labor Day that year was one of those muggy dog days that remind Vermonters how lucky they are not to live farther south. The hamlet of West Brookfield consists of about ten houses sprinkled around a tiny church and a converted one-room schoolhouse. Steep hills slope up both sides of a mile-long valley, whose two hundred acres belong to a single dairy farm. Sheep graze on the hillsides, and on this day smoke was rising from Morris's barbecue pit where two of their fellows were roasting.

I stowed the case of assorted entries from Burlington and took my place at the starting line for the eight-mile race. At 10:00 a.m. sharp, thirty runners started off from under a makeshift banner stretched between two dead elms. It was a tough race, four miles straight up the valley to drain the lungs and four miles straight down to pulverize the knees and Achilles tendons. Steve Morris and I ran as twins to finish in a dripping, respectable fifty-seven minutes.

We were ready for beer. Twenty two people had provided twenty-eight entries. We picked judges on the spot, the only proviso being that none could pass judgment on his own beer.

Morris had printed up some slips of paper with sought-for criteria: head, aroma, taste, aftertaste. We made up the rules and a scoring system as we went along. Our five categories were light ale, dark ale, lager, stout, and Sleazo. The last-named honored Cram Hill brewer Stanley Leon, who, through many years of lonely and difficult labor, had perfected an infamous local concoction named Stanley's Sleazo. Local wags defined it as "the mostest with the leastest." By definition, the Sleazo category contained anything the brewer desired as long as he was committed to the cheapest possible ingredients and the fastest brewing time. Usually this meant Blue Ribbon malt as a base, then whatever sugars were around (cane, molasses, honey, or maple syrup), baker's yeast, and any flavoring from ginger root to vanilla extract. The beer would sit for perhaps three to four days in a single fermenter and then go into containers; these could be screw-top bottles, plastic cider jugs, or whatever was available. If ever there was a beer designed to recall the explosive effervescence of Prohibition, this was it.

I think we started with twelve judges. There seemed to be a strong inverse relationship between the desire to judge and brewing experience.

We tried to give the novices a quick course in bitterness versus sourness, malt flavor versus cider, and sipping versus slurping. But within fifteen minutes, the judging had become pretty free-form . . . and free-foam. At least a third of the bottles were so overprimed that they spewed their contents over judges, notebooks, and observers indiscriminately. One of these beers was actually named Stand Back Lager.

As the afternoon wore on and the novelty wore off, some of the fair-weather judges passed their pencils to unsuspecting friends and slunk off to eat lamb, drink commercial beer, and play volleyball.

Unquestionably, the toughest category was Sleazo. I know because I judged it. Some of those entries were, as H. L. Mencken once said of President Harding's prose, "so awful that a certain grandeur crept in." One tasted simply like vinegar. Another reeked of apple cider gone bad. I sprayed my chest with the contents of one entry. Another produced so much foam that I never did get a taste. And one was so yeasty I felt I'd been dunked in a vat of sourdough. With each sip, I dreaded the next entry more.

The balm for the worst hangover in many years was my victory in the stout category. Peter Seybolt won the lager class with his first-ever batch. The prizes included a modern Stroh's beer tray, a case of old glass bottles, an American Homebrewers Association T-shirt, and one of the first beer cans ever made (1934), from Kreuger Ale in Virginia. Steve Morris had found a case of these cans in an abandoned garage. Printed on the can were instructions on how to use an opener. Since we got to choose our prizes, I picked the can. I later found out that to collectors it is worth over $50.

Last and (very much) least, Charlie Page of Randolph, a man whose style of beermaking a friend described as "turning over rocks to find something interesting to add to the beer," won a bottle of Ripple for his winning Sleazo entry.

A week later, a local television reporter called me to ask if he could tape a short segment about home brewing. He brought his electronic entourage of video, lights, microphones, and fixed questions: How often does a bottle blow up? How strong is the beer? Are you worried about raids from ATF agents? Dressed in American Homebrewers Association T-shirts, Barton Merle-Smith and I demonstrated our equipment in my kitchen. The camera made a sweep of the shelf holding over seventy-five different bottles and cans of imported and better domestic beers (including the Kreuger can), which made the room look like a college dormitory.

I fantasized that a two-minute spot on television would recruit platoons of home brewers to help free the innocent from subjection to Big Brewer. Like any social climber, I didn't hesitate to proclaim my new title, Vermont State Stout Champion, at the slightest opportunity. At the same time, I felt again those itches of boredom, which I had noticed after mastering Grand Rapids lager. I was like the novice sky-diver who tires of static line jumps as he dreams of free-fall. The more I read *Zymurgy* and *Amateur Brewer* (an advanced home brewing newsletter from Portland, Oregon), the more I was convinced that first-class brewing went far beyond malt extracts and hops pellets.

To reach that special state of grace and accomplishment, I had to enter the world of "all-grain brewing." It required learning techniques I had only read about, like mashing, sparging, and water treatment. I had never seen anyone actually make all-grain beer, as it is called. My beers were all-malt, because I used no rice, wheat, or other substitutes. But "all-grain" for advanced brewers means grinding the malted barley, mashing it, and straining out the sugars (sparging), all to get to the point where an extract brewer opens a can of malt syrup or a bag of powdered malt.

Since leaving Grand Rapids and Nichols's store, I had made a habit of visiting home brewing suppliers wherever I found them. One of those was Winemakers Supplies in Northampton, Massachusetts, owned by Frank Romanowski.

Romanowski had been a baker who, fifteen years earlier, began making his own wine. This led him to stocking and selling home winemaking supplies. In a few years, the winemaking business exceeded that of the bakery. He sold the latter and expanded his wares to include beermaking supplies. At the same time, he started brewing himself. Whereas Nichols's customers were primarily interested in the simplest and most reliable ingredients and recipes, Romanowski encouraged his customers to experiment. His store was a bit smaller than Nichols's, but it seemed to have both more equipment and a greater variety of ingredients: six kinds of hops, for example. Romanowski and his wife ran the business with the help of George Peppard (not the actor), who had worked for four months at an English brewery and had dreams of opening his own place in nearby Easthampton.

On my second trip to Northampton, Romanowski offered some of his own pale ale. It was superb—smooth, mellow, and as good as any English bitter I had ever drunk. "This is all-grain beer," he said. "No matter how hard you try, you simply cannot duplicate this with extracts, because extracts cannot provide enough body." My beer was obviously thinner and superficial by comparison.

Again, the past was prologue. I *had* to make all-grain beer. Impatient brewer that I am, I didn't bother to question Romanowski about the technique. I assumed the admirable Burch would tell me all about it in his book. I bought twenty pounds of "two-row" barley and declined Romanowski's offer to grind it for an extra 10 cents per pound.

At home, the first task therefore was to grind the barley, but I now realized I had no idea how fine to make it. I remembered reading somewhere about just cracking the husk. In a section on "Mashing for Flavor," Burch recommended grinding grain with a rolling pin, a coffee grinder, or a blender. Five messy minutes with a rolling pin sent me to the coffee grinder. Using its coarsest setting, I finished the job in twenty minutes, and left a fine layer of grain dust on every horizontal surface of the kitchen.

"Relax. Don't worry. Have a homebrew," I said to myself. I moved on to Burch's one-page section on "Advanced Mashing Techniques." He said that British books on the subject were misleading for Americans, because British malts are more "modified," or converted to fermentable sugars. "With American grain malts," he warned, "you must go through some additional steps not necessary with their British counterparts. The mash is first raised to 95–100 degrees F. and held for one hour. Raise it again to 135 degrees and hold for 20–30 minutes. Raise it then to 150 degrees and hold for 45–60 minutes. Finally, raise it to 170 degrees for ten minutes prior to sparging."

For the first time, I realized that this was not going to be easy. Having already turned the kitchen into a flour mill, I then discovered that the pot I'd used for my previous batches could not hold more than half the grains and the accompanying water. This sent me to the neighbors' for a bigger pot. Burch was unclear about how much water to use, and I made an executive decision to hold the mess-mash to the consistency of half-cooked oatmeal. I kept track of the temperature increases with a candy thermometer.

Four hours later, I finished the boiling portion of Burch's recipe. I tested for starch with a drop of iodine on several drops of mash water. The solution turned brown, not blue, which indicated that all the starches had been converted to sugars. I was ready to sparge, or rinse, all the sugars off the grains and make the resulting liquid the basis of the wort. This would become my substitute for the can of malt extract.

Burch told me to "pour off the free liquid." He suggested several sparging equipment arrangements: a vegetable steamer basket, a camp cooler, or two plastic pails fitted together, the inner one punched full of small holes. I opted for the strainer, because it was all I had. Meanwhile, I realized I would have to heat five to six gallons of water for sparging, and again my brew kettle wouldn't be big enough. Like a beleaguered military commander pressing the cooks and clerks into service, I recruited our eight-gallon enamel canner. The canner was so large that it covered two stove burners.

I hung the strainer basket inside the biggest bowl I had. Then, with a two-quart saucepan, I ladled the grains into the strainer and sprinkled some of my 160° water from the canner over them. One quart of water for one quart of grains seemed reasonable. I tossed the spent grains into a bucket for later deposit on the compost heap.

The sparging operation lasted at least an hour. When I had collected a total of five and a half gallons of potato-colored water, I poured it back into the canner, added the first charge of hops, and turned up the heat. Waiting for it to boil gave me time to clean up the floor, extra pots and pans, spoons, ladles, and other brewing debris.

Just as I was finishing the mop-up and was on my way to the basement with some pans, I heard a hiss of liquid striking fire. I rushed up the steps to see a greenish slime snaking out from under the canner lid and down the side. One burner was already extinguished, and the air was thick with the smell of burnt sugar. I turned off the second burner to assess the damage. It took me fifteen minutes to clean up the sticky mess. In twenty batches of beer, this was the first boil-over I had experienced. I swore it would be the last. Thirty minutes later, I finished the boil, turned off the heat, and added the aromatic hops.

I scooped out a half-pint of wort and placed it in the refrigerator freezer to cool so I could take a hydrometer reading. Then I carried the entire canner to the basement and put it outside in subfreezing temperatures to cool.

It was time to test the original gravity. Two different kinds of degrees here make for confusion. Degrees of extract measure the amount of sugars extracted from the malt or corn sugar and now contained in solution. The hydrometer gives you the density or gravity of the liquid. It is calibrated to read correctly at 60° F. (All new hydrometers contain a chart listing corrections for temperature variations.)

Burch wrote that pale malted barley should give roughly twenty-four gravity degrees per pound of grain. I had ten pounds. Ten times twenty-four equals 240, divided by five eventual gallons of beer, would give me an original gravity of 1048, *IF* I had done everything according to Hoyle.

I cooled a cup of wort to 60° F. by placing it in the deep freeze. Then I poured the contents into the hydrometer's plastic tube. I shook the liquid to get rid of the bubbles and peered at the meniscus. It read . . . 1024 I shook the instrument again and rubbed my eyes. It was still 1024. That was fifteen degrees below even my lowest estimate. I was deeply disappointed. No, I was angry, at Fate, at myself. It made little difference. To spend ten hours, create havoc in the kitchen, and have such thin beer for my pains, was mortifying.

No matter how low the reading, I was damned if I would throw out that batch of beer. I scooped out a gallon of the still-steaming wort, added two pounds of dried malt extract, dissolved it well, boiled it for ten minutes, and poured it back into the primary fermenter. That brought the number of extract degrees to about 1038 or 1040. I knew I was cheating, but how else could I save it?

The next morning, the temperature of the wort had dropped to 80° F. and I added two packets of yeast. Six hours later, fermentation had begun.

During the next few weeks, I thought about that day's work. What conceivable economic, aesthetic, social, culinary, or egoistic benefit could possibly derive from so much messy labor?

At first I wanted to blame Burch. Why hadn't he given more space to the complexities of mashing, made his language clearer, told his readers they would be joining a religious order, not just making a confession? To be fair, his book was for the average novice brewer. When I reread the "Advanced Mashing Techniques" section, I saw it was only meant to be an outline, not a recipe or detailed description. I then realized that mashing is a complex and time-consuming procedure and that I would have to seek advice elsewhere.

When I tasted my first mashed ale, some six weeks later, it did have a bit more body and smoothness than my extracts, but it also had two pounds of dried malt extract that wasn't supposed to be there. There was certainly no hint of greatness.

I added up the pros and cons of sticking to extracts. Romanowski's all-grain beer was 75 to 100 percent better than any extract I had ever made, and it seemed likely that my mashing-sparging technique could be improved with better equipment. I thought I should be able to cut the time from ten hours to seven, or three times what an extract brew required. Was it worth it?

I determined to be more efficient and shorten the brewing time before answering that question.

"Who Brews . . . and Why?"

In the summer of 1981, while leafing through a copy of *The New Republic* in search of liberal answers to the world's problems, I came upon a feature called "Nick's Picks," a column of stock choices by writer Nicholas Von Hoffman. In this article Von Hoffman expatiated on the marvelous "up-side potential" of several beer company equities, notably Anheuser-Busch.

Inflamed with home-brewing self-righteousness, I dashed off the following rejoinder:

With respect to "A Fool and His Money: Slots and Suds" I plead guilty to Von Hoffman's label of a "downcast liberal who doesn't believe in Reaganomics," but there he and I part company, at least on the subject of beer stocks.

At the cost of a single share of Anheuser-Busch stock (selling then at $35), Von Hoffman could buy the basic paraphernalia and ingredients to make, bottle and cap two cases of his own beer or ale. In less than six weeks, his beer/ale would rise spectacularly (in quality) while Bud, Schlitz, Coors and Miller would remain unchanged.

Why are people in rural Vermont paying $4.50 a six-pack for Moosehead or Molson's from Canada, Foster's from Australia, or even Heineken? It's because, as Mike Royko once suggested, "Most American beer tastes as if it had been brewed through a horse."

It costs me about $11 to brew two cases of excellent lager, ale or stout. It would take more than Clydesdales to drag me back to that bland, tasteless liquid that passes for most commercial beer in this country.

Subsequently, the letter appeared on the correspondence page of *TNR* under the subheading "A Better Brew." I was surprised and pleased when, over the next several weeks, I received three phone calls and seven letters from readers across the country—New York, Massachusetts, Georgia, Washington, Arizona, and Texas. Several were already home brewers and just wrote to say "Amen." Others asked me to help them realize "the quality-enhancing potential of home brewing," as one woman wrote. A man from Massachusetts agreed that "A good beer is hard to come by. What can I do about it?"

Whenever the correspondents asked for information, I suggested a couple of texts and a subscription to *Zymurgy*. I was fascinated that this simple letter, penned in humor and ill-humor, had aroused such interest in a political/literary journal. If these readers were excited, what about the thousands (or millions?) of people who drank imported beers regularly, or college students, or good cooks generally? Might they also be converts to home brew?

Who are the home brewers of this world?

I took another look at some of the members of our home brewing club, the Green Mountain Mashers: Anne Whyte, economist; John Gallagher, futon store manager; Maarten VanRyckevorsel, toy-maker's representative; Dan Hament, veterinarian; Paul Hale, chemist; Tom Ayres, brewing store owner; Alden Bee, machinist; Rich Evans, engineer; Lew Greitzer, computer programmer; Tom Walters, sound engineer; Leonard Perry, professor of horticulture.

All of them are professionals, people who have enough money to drink imported beer if they choose. They are discriminating, not heavy, drinkers. Their educated taste buds come from dissatisfaction with largely undifferentiated American beers, from travel abroad, and from curiosity about the imports on store shelves. Some are drawn to home brew's superior taste and natural ingredients, others to the fun of experimentation, and others to a pride in their own creativity. Some are as competitive as can be. Others *never* enter contests and happily brew their simple extract beers month-in and month-out.

There is no single reason why people brew their own beer, any more than there is a single reason why people collect Depression glass, raise show dogs, or fish. I list a number of these reasons below, but I hasten to note that, like vines on a wall, the motivations are often intertwined.

The most common reason for making home brew is a genuine love of good beer. In the early years of the home brewing revolution, home brewers were simultaneously angry about the vapid, homogenized taste of the major American brands and pained by the high price and erratic freshness of the imports. Today, says one local home brewer, "We have absolutely stopped buying imported beers. If I buy beer, it's made by American micro-breweries. They are fresher, more flavorful and usually cheaper than the imports."

Heightened concern about food ingredients and additives drives another cadre of home brewers. Beer has been one of the last classes of food to resist public demands for "natural" ingredients. For years, the brewing industry fought off all attempts to require it to list ingredients on the label. Permissible additives were tabulated in the Congressional Record, but ordinary beer drinkers had no way of knowing what propylene glycol alginate, gallo-tannin, and sodium reythorbate do to their beers; and even if they did, they would still have to wonder why decent beer should require all these foaming agents, stabilizers, color enhancers, and clarifiers. Today, home brewers as well as many micro-brewers follow the Reinheitsgebot (the medieval German Purity Law) and use only malt, hops, water, and yeast.

Experimentation and craftsmanship are the closely related, if not quite synonymous, characteristics of a third class of brewers. On the one hand, there are those who love to experiment with different malts and hops to explore different tastes. Like Paul Angerhofer of the Washington, D.C., brewing club BURP (Brewers United for Real Potables), these people "never make the same beer twice." The panoply of ingredients, techniques, and styles has brought extraordinary choice to the brewing community.

The other form of craftsmanship is expressed in technical virtuosity. Hal Boutelier, one of my mentors, has never stopped experimenting. He takes one bit of information out of this book, another from that fellow brewer, a third from manipulation of his ingredients, and writes it all down. He knows the old methods of brewing were too primitive and inexact, and he is determined to correct that. The chemist Paul Hale has built an entire stainless-steel "brew house" from fifteen-gallon kegs. Add in pumps, two propane burners, mash tun, kegs, and laboratory-level procedures in his brewery, graced by over four hundred different beer bottles and cans, and you have the workshop of a gentle fanatic, whose stout won a third place in the National Homebrewing Competition. These brewers want to stand as close as possible to the fire of commercial brewing without being consumed.

Another category of home brewers is less adventuresome. They work hard to develop and refine a couple of "house brands." They want a steady supply of beer, rather as they want a neat pile of firewood and a crop of ripe tomatoes. For them brewing is one of several hobbies, not the alpha and omega of their lives.

Although Ninkasi, the Sumerian beer deity, was female, and the word *brewster* originally meant "woman brewer," female brewers are still relatively rare. But their numbers are growing. Anne Whyte is president of the Green Mountain Mashers. "I have always liked good beers. I started to think about brewing my own when I saw a newspaper article about this guy in Albany who wanted to build a brewery. I vowed that if I ever won the lottery, that is what I would do with it. After I took a course in home brewing, I was hooked. I think it was my love of making things that got me into this. I was a baker. I learned when to follow the recipe and when you could wing it. I like to experiment with ingredients and techniques.

"One of the problems women brewers face is how to get information and guidance. My husband's a builder and I watch how he teaches apprentices. It's a real hands-on, word-of-mouth tradition. Beermaking is like that. Brewers learn a lot from their buddies, and I don't have any buddies I can hang out with except in the club."

Anne gets sympathy from AHA founder Charlie Papazian. "Ninety-seven percent of our members are men. A major part of brewing is the camaraderie, the information exchange, the male rapport. It's a lot harder for women to feel comfortable in places where there is all this 'guy talk.' But it's progressing. More assertive women are going to clubs to make their feelings known. The Great American Beer Festival now draws about forty percent women."

Jokingly, Anne suggests that women ought to brew more. "I've told my single women friends that, if you want to meet interesting guys, this is a great place to do it. They are clever, responsible, probably good cooks and good conversationalists. They drink in moderation *and* they know how to clean up."

(Throughout this book, I have used the male pronoun to describe the average home brewer, simply because far more men than women practice this hobby. No slight is intended.)

Comradeship is integral to brewing. Although most brewers brew alone, the sharing of triumphs and tragedies, of curiosity and insight, of nonbrewing interests and ideas—not to mention the beer itself—draws the brewers together. Clubs serve for the exchange of information and beer. The Green Mountain Mashers are so organized they have agendas for their monthly meetings. They take field trips to area breweries and sponsor competitions. Yet they also work hard to make all feel welcome, especially novice brewers.

One final class of home brewers is what beer writer Fred Eckhardt calls "the cheap beer crowd." They are cousins of most English home brewers. That is, their prime motivation is economic. With huge excise taxes on alcoholic beverages, English home brewing is largely a financial necessity. In this country, the "CBC" may drink a lot, have little money, or both. This group doesn't want anything fancy, just simple ingredients and a straightforward recipe. Boil it, cool it, get the yeast in, ferment it for a few days, and fill those bottles. Age it for a couple of weeks and drink it down.

A related category consists of the thrill-seekers. They love to boost the alcohol content, usually by adding cheap corn sugar. Such a practice was widespread during Prohibition, when people were more interested in getting hammered than in brewing fine beer. This subspecies of swaggering, often staggering brewers embarrass their more serious brethren. They love to brag about their beer with 8 to 10 percent alcohol content. Legally, this is not beer but malt liquor, although, with its high percentage of nonmalt sugars, it isn't even much of a malt beverage. Finally, unlike almost all brewers, these cheap beermakers don't share their beer. Fortunately, this subset is probably small. Tom Ayres, founder of two home brew clubs and co-owner of two retail stores, says he knows probably a thousand home brewers firsthand and not one would he count an alcoholic. If you decide you want to "get wasted" tonight, you are not going to wait a month or two to drink the agent of your wasting.

Most brewers want external recognition to go with internal pride. Like me, a brewer might want a personal label. With an artist friend I traded two six-packs of stout for a label design which, befitting my name, showed the rear end of a horse. At first, home brewers may be a bit insecure and hesitant to offer their beer. They may even deride their beer first, on the principle of the French aphorist La Rochefoucauld: "We confess to little faults to persuade ourselves [and others] we have no great ones." But then the mantle of modesty comes off like Clark Kent's civvies in a phone booth, and you can't shut them up. Someone once jokingly said to me: "Mares, I don't know which is worse, when you were good company and your beer was lousy, or now, when your beer is good and you talk of little else."

The spread of home brewing competitions across the country, spurred by the American Homebrewers Association, has given home brewers a marvelous venue for public acclaim.

Even without the ribbons and cups of home brewing championships, however, most home brewers have a proselytizing streak, an active desire to convert the heathen still drinking standard American beer. In the gentle words of J. I. Rodale, founder of *Organic Gardening*, speaking of his discovery of composting: "I felt I had to share this experience with the rest of the country. It would not be fair to know this and say nothing about it."

Such a true-believing home brewer may face a conundrum. He can't expect to convert the confirmed "light"-beer drinker without giving him something close to what he is accustomed to. And if a light-beer drinker actually likes your beer, you might wonder if it's flavorful enough. The point here is similar to that of Groucho Marx's famous line, "I wouldn't want to belong to any club which would have me as a member." A brew that appeals to everyone is necessarily an undistinguished brew. The solution is to be guided by your own tastes and preferences; that way, you will have at least one satisfied customer. And if you are devoted to light beer, you probably should not brew your own. It will have too much taste for you.

Not only do brewers love to give away their beer, they are not above joining the underground economy of barter. John Gallagher traded some home brew for a radiator installation. Anne Whyte exchanged her beer for some vegetables and a salsa recipe. And I have "bought" fishing advice with some of my ale.

Brewing, like winemaking, gives the maker pride of accomplishment, the savor of possession, and the warmth of sharing. How do I know about all these different reasons for brewing? Because at one time or another, I have acutely experienced them all.

Ingredients

Once again, a choice was at hand. I could stick to my extracts and experiment *ad infinitum* with different hops and malt syrups or crystal grain and maintain my current production of two cases every four to six weeks. In four years, I had found or developed three brews—a lager, an ale, and a stout—which I (and most of our guests) liked. My talents were publicly recognized through a victory in the home brew championships. As long as I kept my mouth shut, no one but Chris would know of my all-grain disaster. What's more, all-grain brewing and bottling took most of a day. Even if I calculated my time as low as $6.00 an hour and the ingredients at $20, all-grain brew would still cost roughly $1.20 a bottle. I could drink Heineken or Guinness for that.

But I was not part of the cheap-beer crowd. I didn't brew because home brew was less expensive than the store-bought variety. I was in love with the seductive aroma, and the taste of real beer. I delighted in the *process* of making beer. And extracts were beginning to bore me. Despite my failure, I knew that the taste of mashed beer was no mirage. Hal Boutelier and other grain brewers made superb beers. Getting there would take longer and required more preparations, but maybe it seemed worth it. I realized I was generally happier wrestling with a new problem than coasting on a past solution.

Ever the pragmatist, Chris said that, if I was committed to making better beers, I needed to learn more about the ingredients and tools of brewing. Sound advice.

From home brew stores, friends, the University of Vermont library, and mail-order houses, I collected a dozen British and American professional and home brewing manuals. These volumes varied widely in detail, emphasis, and, alas, accuracy. If I got angry at myself for stupid or perverse brewing mistakes, I was equally incensed by the confusing directions, oversimplification, and misinformation (I couldn't call them "lies") some of these books offered. One modestly promised to teach all you needed to know about making beer . . . in forty-two pages. Another defined ale and lager without any reference to the types of yeast employed. Some said one needn't boil the wort. Turning to the professional texts to mediate the squabbles was of little help; they were often too detailed for this lay reader. The sad conclusion I reached was that Professors Trial and Error would be teaching my graduate course in brewing.

In between the brewing texts, I read some more brewing history. From Michael Jackson's* lush *World Guide to Beer,* I learned that the most important date in the evolution of the beverage was probably the year 1516. One year before Martin Luther nailed his ninety-five theses on the court church door at Wittenberg and launched the Protestant Reformation, there occurred in Bavaria an event of similar gravity. Needing money for a military campaign, the Elector of that duchy decided to use the brewing industry as a source of revenue. To that end, he had to distinguish Bavarian beer from its host of competitors. He chose purity over adulteration. The Reinheitsgebot, or Purity Law, stipulated that Bavarian beer could contain only malted barley, hops, and water. (The yeast was assumed, though not named.) This law was adhered to in most of Germany for almost five centuries and did as much as anything to preserve a worldwide standard of beer quality and excellence. (The Reinheitsgebot, having survived plagues and countless wars, finally fell victim to European economic union as other nations forced Germany to open their taps to brews less rigorously made. However, purity of ingredients has become a hallmark of many of the new micro-brewers in this country.)

Twenty-six years after promulgation of the Reinheitsgebot, in a book called *A Compendious Regyment or a Dyetary of Health* (1542), the Englishman Andrew Boorde wrote: "Ale is made of malte and water; and

---

* Not the best-known one, needless to say.

they the which do put any other thynge to ale than is rehearsed, except yest, barme, or godesgood, doth sofysticate theyr ale." Unfortunately, Boorde was only a commoner, and his injunction never attained the force of law.

Enough digression. It's on to the ingredients.

BARLEY

Barley is a grain with multiple uses in cereals, soups, and cattle feed, but its primary value lies in brewing. Raw barley cannot be transformed directly into alcohol. The starches in the grains must first be converted into fermentable sugars on which the yeast works to produce alcohol and carbon dioxide.

Barley is either two-row or six-row, depending upon the configuration of the kernels on the stalk. The former has a higher starch content, paler color, and fewer enzymes. The latter has less starch and more enzymes. About 80 percent of American-grown barley is six-row. By using this strain of barley, American brewers historically were able to harness excess enzymes to convert starches in other grains, such as rice and corn, thus producing a lighter, clearer, and more stable beer.

The first step in this conversion process is malting, which the professional brewing manual *The Practical Brewer* defines as "the controlled germination of barley during which enzymes are formed and food reserves (starches) are sufficiently modified so they can be further hydrolyzed (dissolved) during mashing." The malting process is too complex and time-consuming for all but a tiny number of home brewing fanatics. In fact, in this country, only Coors and some of the older Budweiser breweries do their own malting. All the rest are customers of huge malting companies.

The malting of barley occurs in three stages: steeping the raw grain, partial germination, and drying. The process lasts from five to twelve days, depending upon the kind of barley and the variety of malt sought. During germination, the starch portion of the grain is softened and made porous, and enzymes are distributed throughout. The beer's final aroma and color are determined during the drying, or kilning, phase. The higher the temperature, the darker the color and more "roasted" the aroma.

Think of the maltster as a cross between a drill instructor and a quartermaster. Through a careful mixture of time, temperature, and moisture, he trains and supplies his enzyme and starch troops, turning them into ready warriors in the cause of good beer.

The range of malts available to the home brewer today is as varied as that for the professional brewer. Two friends of mine who run retail brewing shops offer fifteen to seventeen different kinds of malt from the U.S., England, Germany, and Belgium. This is three times the number of malts I could get fifteen years ago. What's more, the malts are fresh and are sold according to a professional color scale called the "Lovibond rating."

The major malts are:

Pale malt.   The most common and widely used malt, dried at a temperature of around 175° F., which stops germination without killing the enzymes. This malt provides at least 95 percent of the fermentable sugars for the average grain brew.

Caramel or crystal malt.   Partially dried, rewetted with a sugary water, then heated to 250° F. Some fermentable sugars are developed during this process, but, more important, the heat caramelizes the outer coating and gives the beer a rich, nutty flavor and a darker, even reddish glow.

Chocolate malt.   Malt roasted to a dark-brown (chocolate) color. Retains a slightly sweet and toasted flavor.

Black patent malt.   Malt roasted at a temperature above 450° F., thus driving off all aroma. Used chiefly for coloring beer, notably stouts.

Roasted barley.   Made by roasting unmalted barley at high temperatures to give the toasted flavor and deep-brown color of roasted coffee beans.

Dextrin (Cara-pils) malt.   Must be mashed with other enzyme-supplied grains. Aids in head retention and fuller body.

Vienna and Munich malts.   These European malts add an amber color to beer and impart their own distinctive flavors, depending upon how much you use.

ADJUNCTS

If you use dextrose for more than priming, you are adding an "adjunct" to the malt. Adjuncts are any substitute unmalted cereal grain or fermentable ingredient added to the mash. According to *The Practical Brewer*, "Adjunct use results in beers of lighter color, with a less satiating, snappier taste, greater brilliance, enhanced physical stability and superior chill-proof qualities . . . attributes extremely important with packaged beers."

I used to believe a conspiracy theory that American beer had become progressively weaker and more adulterated with nonbarley adjuncts simply because the big brewers found they could make more money that way, and the public was too dumb to know the difference. I've grown a bit wiser. Certainly, profit is still paramount in their eyes. But I think the customers also wanted a less filling and clearer beer. To achieve that meant cutting down on the calories, alcohol, and body.

Most major American beers contain between 30 and 40 percent adjuncts. Some of these substitutes are corn grits, flaked barley, oats, and wheat, but the big two are corn and rice. I don't see a need for any grains besides malt and occasionally wheat. However, in Charlie Papazian's witty and encyclopedic *New Complete Joy of Home Brewing*, there are dozens of additional ingredients for making offbeat beers—syrups, fruits, vegetables, honey, spices, herbs.

A word about wheat. Until the 1980s, the only places in the world to drink wheat beers were Belgium and Germany. The home brewing/microbrewing revolution during that decade brought that distinct style to the United States. But where the European wheat beers had a fruitiness born of special yeasts and fermentation practices, the Americans sometimes used lager or ale yeast to produce a beer closer to traditional lagers or ales. Wheat beers rarely contain more than 50 percent wheat—the rest is usually barley.

OTHER INGREDIENTS

Finings. Various organic or mineral substances used to ensure that haze-forming substances, like yeast cells, proteins, and other suspended matter, coagulate and settle to the bottom of the fermentation vessel. Two of the most prominent exemplars are *Irish Moss* and *gelatin*.

Malto-dextrins.   These nonfermentable malt sugars add body, stability, and some additional sweetness to beer.

Gypsum.   Calcium sulphate. Helps in mashing, and to clarify beer by precipitating out proteins, tannins, and husk flavors.

WATER

Extract brewers need not worry too much about the kinds of water they use, as long as it tastes and smells okay.

   With all-grain brewing, water takes on more importance, and the first rule about it offends common sense: don't use the distilled variety. One would think that pure mineral-free water would be a perfect alternative to questionable wells or inconsistent public supplies. Unfortunately, purity in brewing water is not rewarded, as I found out to my woe when I brewed a couple of batches in Grand Rapids and got a weak feckless product for my trouble. Good beer requires minerals.

   Mashing, boiling, and fermentation are chemical reactions that depend upon certain chemical constituents of the water in which they occur. The mashing reaction should take place under slightly acidic conditions, between 5.2 and 5.7 pH, because those are the optimum conditions for the release and work of the enzymes. Since most municipal water is close to neutrality, or 7.0 pH, the brewer needs to lower the pH (raise the acidity). The principal chemical reaction occurs when gypsum reacts with phosphorus in the malt to produce calcium phosphate, which settles out, and phosphorous acid, which encourages mashing reactions.

   Don't lose sight of your goal: to make good beer. You can drive yourself nuts exploring some of the arcana of water treatment. You are not running a chemical laboratory. People, including yourself, who drink the beer care about the taste and the appearance. After years of experimenting with different water treatments, I have concluded that the KISS principle (Keep It Simple, Stupid) works best. Assuming that I use municipal water (Burlington's has improved markedly of late) that is roughly neutral, I add two teaspoons of gypsum to five gallons of water for pale ales and lagers, one teaspoon for porters and steam beers, and none for stouts. The amount of gypsum varies with the batch, because the darker malts already possess adequate acidity and therefore may be brewed with softer water.

It is good to remember the words of Professor Michael Lewis, who teaches fermentation science at the University of California at Davis. "Many people get hung up on water treatment when they should be working on their sanitation problems. *That*, not water, is something they really can affect."

HOPS

Until I started brewing, my sole mental association with hops came from George Orwell's essay on hop-picking in Kent during the Depression—a grim account of long hours, exploitation, miserable wages, and physical discomfort. There was not one word about drinking or making beer. "One's hands get stained as black as a negro's with the hop juice, which only mud can remove, and after a day or two they crack and are cut to bits by the (spiny) stems of the vines." For his labor, Orwell earned 10 shillings, or about $2.00, a week.

Hops turn simple, sweet beer into complex and bitter ambrosia. The first use of hops resulted from brewers' restless search for different flavors and, more important later, for substances that would sterilize and preserve their fragile beverage. Hops have been used in brewing since the thirteenth century, but until about 150 years ago their most prominent quality was that of a soporific, and people stuffed them in pillows to get a better sleep.

Hops are members of the same biological family as *Cannabis sativa* (marijuana), but lack the latter's mind-altering powers. Long found wild in most temperate climates, hops are a perennial, bisexual vine with a phenomenal growing capacity, sometimes six inches a day. When cultivated, they are trained along wires or trellises and may rise thirty feet in a season.

For the brewer, the important part of the plant is the female flower. These green cones (or strobiles) are roughly the size of acorns and look like pineapples. In brewing, they serve three functions:

1. In their yellow lupulin powder lie the alpha and beta resins, which provide bitterness and a sterilizing quality to the beer. They are released during the vigorous boiling cycle. They retain no odor, and settle out during the subsequent fermentation.

2. The essential oils impart a distinctive aroma for each variety of hops. This flavor is destroyed during the boil. Therefore, some hops are always added to the wort at the end of the boil, so the aroma may be gently released and trail off during fermentation and aging. When I keg beer, I usually add a half-ounce of loose hops or pelletized hops to the keg.

The brewer divides hops into two classes: boiling, or bittering hops; and flavoring, aromatic, or finishing hops. The freshest hops should be used for flavoring.

3. Hops also contain tannins that coagulate with the haze-forming proteins and carry them to the bottom during the boil and fermentation.

Hops are marketed in four forms: loose, pellets, oils, and plugs. Loose hops are stripped from the vines, and packed in two-hundred-pound bales, or "pockets." Home brewers wanting fresh hops should look for the following characteristics: the color should be green or greenish yellow, with lemon-colored lupulin powder evident; the aroma should be clean without any earthy or sulfury smell; the texture should be springy, not crackly or mushy, and have a smooth "rub." Your friends may be impressed to hear you are using Saaz or Styrian loose, but if the hops have spent two years in the hold of the *Flying Dutchman,* you are fooling no one but yourself.

Hops pellets are merely whole hops which have been chopped and pulverized in a mill and then pelletized. Hop oils are available but are difficult to use, because they are not soluble in water or beer. Hops plugs are compressed loose hops in one-half-ounce units (about the size of a stack of five half-dollar pieces) in vacuum-sealed packages.

Evidence of the increasing sophistication of home brewing shows up in the marketing of hops. Ten years ago, there were recipes which called indiscriminately for "two ounces" of three or four kinds of hops, as if all were the same in flavor, *and* in strength. Today, most reputable brewing supply retailers mimic professional brewers by denoting the "alpha acid content" of their hops. It's the alpha acids that supply the bitterness in beer. Through an objective measurement of "homebrew bitterness units," the home brewer can strike the desired balance between sweetness and bitterness in the specific brew.*

One of the great joys of home brewing is the chance to experiment with different flavors and styles. With over a dozen kinds of malt, and a score of hops varieties to choose from, the home brewer has a virtually limitless variety of beers to make. For the traditional brewer, consistency is the greatest virtue. For the home brewer, variety is not only the spice but the very substance of life.

Some of the better-known hops varieties are listed below:

Cluster. Widely used as a "kettle" hop in standard American lagers. Has excellent aroma and stability. About 20 percent of all American hops are clusters. Medium bitterness (5–8 percent alpha acid).

Cascade. Lower bitterness (4–7 percent alpha acid), with a fine flowery aroma.

Willamette. The major American aromatic hop, with about 20 percent of overall production. Very similar to Fuggles, the workhorse of English beers, but with better stability. (Alpha acid 5–7 percent.)

Hallertau. A German lager hop from Bavaria and a firm friend. With its mild but spicy aroma, this hop helped wean me off hopped malt extracts. (Alpha acid 5–7 percent.)

Tettnanger. A cousin of the Hallertau, now grown in the U.S. Low alpha acid (3–4 percent), with nice aroma.

Galena, Eroica, Nugget. Three varieties of the new superalpha hops, developed in the last fifteen years. With alpha acid of 12–15 percent, these are blockbuster bittering hops, and now comprise almost 30 percent of U.S. hops production.

---

* According to Charlie Papazian, homebrew bitterness units (HBU) are calculated by multiplying the percent of alpha acid in the hops by the number of ounces and then dividing that by the number of gallons in the batch to get a per-gallon figure.

Northern Brewer. Fritz Maytag uses this medium alpha acid hop (7–9 percent) for his Anchor Steam Beer.

Saaz. The hops used in perhaps the most famous lager in the world, Pilsner Urquell, and synonymous with Bohemian beers. When fresh, it has a stunningly spicy and pungent taste. Low alpha acid (4–6 percent).

Perle. Useful for both bittering and aroma in lagers. Bred to resemble German Northern Brewer hops. (Alpha acid 7–9 percent.)

As American commercial beer became ever lighter with the use of more adjuncts, the use of hops declined, because the hops were meant to balance the strong malt flavor. With the recent brewing revival, both at home and in micro-breweries, the "hop rate" of beers—at least among these segments of the industry—has returned to appropriate levels. As a hops lover, I couldn't be happier (hoppier?).

If you feel even more adventuresome, you can now grow your own hops.* One can order hops roots (rhizomes) by mail. Or you can be lucky, like our home brew club, the Green Mountain Mashers, and have among your members a university botanist who is doing research on East Coast hops culture. Dr. Leonard Perry grows 14–16 different varieties and shares some of the hops with fellow members in return for their help in harvesting the crop.

YEAST

The translators of the King James Bible called yeast "leaven." The Greeks dubbed it *zestos*, meaning "boiling." Early English brewers called it Godisgood. And the Bavarian Reinheitsgebot didn't even mention it.

Yeast, the magical substance which turns sweet wort into beer, is one of the simplest forms of plant life. This single-celled fungus, through very complex chemical reactions, converts sugars into carbon dioxide and

---

* See David Beach, *Homegrown Hops* (1992), 92984 River Rd., Junction City, OR 97448; and the article on hops in the Special 1990 Issue of *Zymurgy*.

alcohol. (In breadmaking the alcohol is driven off during baking and the carbon dioxide makes the loaf rise.) A single yeast cell may reproduce thirty times before it dies. Over five hundred types of yeast have been isolated, not including the many wild strains that are always present in the air. The brewer is only interested in two varieties: the top-fermenting *Saccharomyces cerevisiae* and the bottom-fermenting *Saccharomycesuvarum*.

Top-fermenting yeast works on the surface of the beer at temperatures between 55° and 80° F. It has a higher alcohol tolerance—that is, it can produce beers with a higher alcohol content. It does not convert dextrins well, so the resulting beers are sweeter. Generally, it is used in English-style ales, porters, and stouts.

Bottom-fermenting yeast is more fragile, works at lower temperatures (down to 33° F.), and has less alcohol tolerance, but it settles more readily, converts dextrins more completely, and makes for a brighter beer. This is the yeast for lagers. Beer writer Michael Jackson suggests that it was the advent of mechanical refrigeration which permitted brewers to sustain the lower temperatures needed for good bottom-fermentation, which, in turn, helped to promote lager, rather than ale, as the more universally popular beverage.

Alcoholic fermentation can take place with or without oxygen. In the presence of oxygen, yeast will rapidly convert sugar into the constituent carbon dioxide and alcohol. In oxygenless conditions, conversion is much slower. For the brewer, the trick is to get the yeast working quickly (with oxygen), then cut off the air supply and let the yeast reproduce throughout the remaining wort without exposure to air. Fermentation will then continue until all the sugars are converted, or the alcohol content has reached a level which inhibits further conversion. The home brewer can easily see the two stages of yeast production. In the primary fermentation, one sees a high, protective head of foam and carbon dioxide. The ale ferment will produce a very craggy head (and higher than that for lagers). In the secondary fermentation, the brewer sees a longer, slower period of conversion.

Breweries live or die by their yeasts. They spend much time and effort culturing and maintaining particular strains. They look for such characteristics as growth, fermenting power, resistance to bacteria, and flocculation property—the ability to latch on to other cells and carry them to the bottom as a sediment. Once commercial breweries have developed a reliable strain of yeast, they will keep using it from batch to batch, until it shows signs of weakening. It's the brewer's equivalent of apostolic succession. Ale brewers normally skim the middle portion of the foamy head for their succeeding batches, whereas lager brewers retrieve their yeast from the bottom of the fermenting vessel.

Even though the readers of this book are amateur brewers, it is worth quoting a passage from *The Practical Brewer* on the subject of yeast contamination: "It is not possible to set fixed limits for the degree of infection which may be tolerated, as the conditions are different in every brewery. It is obvious that the biological purity of yeast goes hand in hand with the cleanliness of the plant and the sterility of the equipment. For that reason it is necessary to employ the strictest cleaning and sanitation procedures in order to establish and maintain practical sterility. This point cannot be stressed enough." If you read further in the manual to learn about the various infections, about bacteria and other airborne nasties, you could be frightened away from brewing altogether.

As with all other ingredients, yeast varieties and quality have improved dramatically in recent years. The principal forms are:

Dry, granulated yeast.   This is the variety most home brewers are familiar with. My preferences are Edme and Williams. I always use two packets for each five-gallon batch, even when a recipe calls for only one. And I make a starter (see below).

Liquid yeasts.   Although two to four times as expensive as the dry yeasts, the liquid forms have greater variety, better taste, and more reliability, I think. Should be used with a starter.

Culture your own.   I have not attempted this, but friends have, successfully. The procedure requires appropriate laboratory equipment, patience, and care. For an article on isolating and culturing yeast from bottle-conditioned beer, see the Special Issue of *Zymurgy*, "Yeast," vol. 12, no. 4 (1989), or Charlie Papazian's *New Complete Joy of Home Brewing*.

Baker's yeast.   What I call Prohibition Pilsner was made with Blue Ribbon hopped malt, cane sugar, and baker's yeast. It imparted a very yeasty taste to the beer, on top of the cidery taste derived from the cane sugar. I suspect that several hundred thousand home brewers to this day are using these materials, because they are not experimenters; they are drinkers.

In the *Zymurgy* issue mentioned above is an interesting article about "Fleischmann's (aka Budweiser) Yeast." The author, Kurt Denke, says the yeast is grown by Anheuser-Busch and is sold in two-pound (!) bricks. With this yeast Denke won a first place in the herb beer category of the AHA National Competition.

Repitch your own.   Before Louis Pasteur, Emil Hansen, and yeast laboratories, there were the *lees*—accumulated yeast, proteins, and hops left as a scummy layer on the bottom of fermentation vessels after the beer was transferred to aging casks. I have had great success in using these lees for subsequent batches. One technique is to leave the lees of one batch in the bottom of my secondary fermenter after bottling and then, because I have brewed at roughly the same time, to pour the cooled wort back into the same carboy. The alternative is to take one or two cups of these lees and add them to the new batch.

To repeat *ad nauseam,* all equipment and conditions need to be as sterile as possible.

Tap your local professional brewer.   I'm lucky. The Vermont Pub and Brewery is a five-minute bike ride from my house. Secondly, Greg Noonan, the owner, is a generous fellow. He lets me come and "borrow" some of his yeast every four or five months. Needless to say, the beer produced with his yeast far surpasses anything I make with the packaged variety. I'm chary of recommending that readers importune professional brewers for yeast, but if you spend some time cultivating that brewer, you never know what might happen. . . .

INFORMATION

Starting a new hobby means venturing into new territory. Without a guide, this can be unsettling, even unnerving. In the years since the first edition of this book appeared, I have had telephone calls from brewers as far away as Arizona and Alaska wanting to know where to buy supplies, or whether they could substitute certain ingredients, or how to drill holes in a sparging bucket, and so on.

In the early days of brewing, most people learned by trial and error exclusively. There were no texts. Friends were often similarly in the dark. The results were problematic. That is no longer the case. We live in the Information Age, goes the cliché, and brewing is no exception.

In the Bibliography, I have listed a number of resources, from texts to magazines and newspapers where you can get more brewing information.

In addition to its quarterly magazine, *Zymurgy*, AHA is producing two or three volumes a year about specific beer styles. You can buy a hundred-plus-page book about Vienna, Belgian Ale, Continental Pilsner, Lambic, Pale Ale, Porter, etc.

I would add a word here about the value of friends. Home brewing clubs are an excellent source of information and camaraderie for the novice brewer. Clubs are, after all, places for the convivial sharing of achievement and experience. As a professional brewer once told me, "There are no secrets in brewing, only your mistakes." If there is a home brewing club nearby, join it. If there isn't, start one.

Just in the last half-dozen years, there have sprung up at least ten "brewspapers" or "beereodicals" which chronicle the beer industry. They report on openings of new breweries and visit existing ones. They cover beer festivals, or do pub tours.

All of these papers are free. They seem to be supported by a mixture of ads from brewing companies, home brew supply outlets, retailers and wholesalers, and various regional beer festivals.

Finally, there is the computer. The personal computer (and modem) are displacing the Postal Service for the many people who want (almost) instant communication. I happen to belong to CompuServe, but there are other brewing forums and libraries in other data banks. When you get onto the network, you can read and write in the forum on wine and beer. Inside the "libraries," you can scroll through recipes, download graphics, including beer labels which someone has copied electronically, ask general questions on home brewing. You can start your own "thread" or conversation. Perhaps you are getting odd smells or tastes from a particular batch and you want to ask a question of someone out there in the electronic ether. You give your thread a name, describe your predicament, then sit back and wait for a comment. It's a bit like setting a trotline for fish. Almost inevitably, and usually fairly quickly, someone or several someones (depending upon how intriguing the question) will jump in with observations, comforting words, suggested solutions, and so on. There are "online beer tastings" where a group will sit down in front of a computer in five different cities, drink the same beer, and comment on its flavor. There are high-level discussions, as when Fritz Maytag, founder of Anchor Brewing Company in San Francisco, sat down at his computer and answered questions sent to him from all across the country. Whereas the magazine editors are cautious about offending product advertisers, such shyness does not afflict those manning the modems. So, if you have a computer and a modem, don't be afraid to join the electronic brewing fraternity.

It is important to remember that good ingredients will not rescue your beer from bad technique, but proper procedures and the right equipment can make up for inferior (though not infected) ingredients. It is to equipment that we now turn.

Equipment

To produce consistently good beer, you don't need to be fancy, but you must possess the proper tools and techniques. With the extraordinary improvements in home brewing equipment and information over the past ten or fifteen years, there is no reason why anyone should fail to make good clean beer on the first or fiftieth batch.

Home brewing equipment may be divided into three classes: that required for good extract brewing; that needed for all-grain brewing; and extras which may be useful or just plain fun to have. These categories reflect degrees of brewing enthusiasm (or fanaticism?).

The 70–80 percent of American home brewers who use extracts want simplicity, flavor, moderate cost, and replicability. They may experiment. The explosion in varieties of ingredients and styles has given extract brewers a choice of beers unimaginable a decade ago. Indeed, some have won national competitions with their beer. But, by and large, the extract brewers expect their hobby to know its place and not overrun the rest of their lives.

The all-grain brewers, too, reach the stage where beermaking is a habit. But they tend to be more restless of mind. They keep looking for ways to improve the beer. They are willing to spend a whole day in brewing, because they are convinced their beer will be significantly better than anything they can buy. Further, they are willing to invest in more elaborate and expensive equipment to assure this triumph. The all-grain brewer is like the bear who goes over the mountain—there is always one more device or technique to see, to buy, or to experiment with.

EQUIPMENT FOR EXTRACT BREWING

Kits.   A warning. There are a number of brewing kits on the market. Their quality ranges widely. The equipment is usually correct for simple beginner's extract batches. The recipes can be misleading. Some will say you don't have to boil the wort. Others, in an effort to keep the price down, will say you need only one can of malt and you can increase the alcohol content with corn sugar. I strongly recommend that, from the first batch, brewers use at least five or six pounds of malt extract in a five-gallon batch, *and* that they boil their wort for at least forty-five minutes.

Boiler.   Despite what some kit directions say, you cannot make decent beer without boiling the primary ingredients. Therefore, you need a vessel of two-to-three-gallon capacity for carrying out the sublime marriage of the sweet wort with the bitter hops. This may be a steamer, a spaghetti cooker, or a soup pot. Stainless steel is the best, and most expensive. I've known of people who use either aluminum or enamel canning pots. I can't recommend the latter. A friend of mine spent two weeks in the hospital with burns suffered when the handles of such a pot full of hot wort broke as he was carrying the batch down a flight of stairs.

Primary fermenter.   This vessel should be at least five or six gallons in size. I strongly recommend glass (see section on **blow-by** below), although many brewers use food-grade plastic buckets happily. My quarrels with plastic are that (a) the buckets can be easily scratched, thus building a home for nefarious bacteria; (b) they are harder to clean; and (c) their tops don't fit as snugly as I prefer.

Secondary fermenter.   To house the quieter, slower second stage of fermentation, the ideal container is a five- or six-gallon glass carboy. If you have glass for a primary fermenter, you may use a second carboy or, as I note below in the discussion of the **blow-by,** you may use the same carboy. These carboys are available in flea markets and home brew shops and cost roughly $25.00.

In twenty years of brewing, I have broken only one carboy—when I employed it as a primary fermenter without first cooling the wort. Senselessly assuming the glass was Pyrex-grade, I poured some 210° F. wort into it. I heard a slight crack, but since none was visible, I poured in the rest of the wort. When it was time to move the carboy closer to the faucet to add water, I lifted all of the carboy . . . except the bottom. The glass had cracked cleanly around the base, leaving only a shallow dish. The hot sticky wort spread across the kitchen floor and under the refrigerator. It took two hours to clean up the mess. Moral: add cool water to the wort first, because a carboy cannot stand direct heat of more than about 140° F.

Incidentally, pay heed to your back when you lift a carboy. It weighs a good fifty pounds when full, and two cases of the best beer hardly compensate for a wrenched back or a hernia. I would recommend buying a carboy handle, to ease the movement of these unwieldy vessels.

Blow-by or blow-off tube.   The main reason I stopped using a plastic fermenting bucket was the advice of Professor Michael Lewis and home brewing technocrat Al Andrews. They taught me to make beer entirely in glass carboys using the "blow-by" technique. A blow-by is nothing more than a four-to-five-foot piece of plastic tubing of one-inch interior diameter (available by the foot at any good hardware store) that is wedged into the top of the carboy and curves down into a bucket of water or chlorine solution.

The blow-by allows the first, turbulent fermentation to blow out through a froth of yeasty, hoppy foam, without permitting air back into the vessel. This process continues for one to three days, depending upon the type of yeast, the temperature of the brew, and how full the carboy is. As little as a pint and as much as two quarts of liquid could pass through the tube. When it is time for secondary fermentation, I either siphon the wort into another, clean carboy or leave it in the original and add a fermentation lock.

The greatest advantage of the blow-by is improvement in sanitation. The beer is not exposed to air except at moments of transfer. Further, the carboy's narrow neck does not tempt you to touch the beer with a possibly contaminated spoon or hydrometer. Finally, by leaving the beer in a single carboy for the entire ferment, you also avoid possible contamination from the transfer to a secondary fermenter.

Fermentation lock. Also called an "airlock" or "bubbler." Hats off to the inventor of this simple device, which allows fermentation to proceed undisturbed by the intrusion of nefarious wild yeasts or other airborne spoilers. Filled with water, the plastic lock permits carbon dioxide to bubble off while excluding the outside air.

In the days before fermentation locks, choosing a time to bottle was an art akin to a farmer's decision on when to plant. Littleton Long and Leonides Jones, both professors of English at the University of Vermont, brewed with the same recipe for over thirty-five years. According to their instructions: "Since there are so many variables, the safest indication of bottling time is the appearance of the brew itself. After the period of scum or foam formation is past, bubbles the size of a pinhead will be seen bursting through the surface and going half an inch in the air. Gradually these will diminish in frequency and in size (to pinpoint dimension) and irregular islands or patches of thin foam will appear on the surface. The bubbling at this stage might best be described as a mist slowly rising to the surface. This is technically called 'allowing the beer to go flat.' Catching the beer at this point calls for judgment based upon several experiences. There is no danger in letting the beer go too flat; the danger lies in bottling too soon, for bottles will explode if the internal pressure becomes too great."

Some brewing texts suggest using a hydrometer to tell when the beer is ready to bottle. I don't. Every time you open your fermenter, you risk some contamination. When the bubbles in the lock come less frequently than once every ninety seconds, I know it's time to bottle. Depending upon the yeast type and the ambient temperature, this might take as little as a week or as long as five weeks. Be patient.

Dark plastic bags. Beer is light-sensitive, which is why most commercial beer bottles are of amber or dark-green glass. Once the beer is in the carboy, I slip a garbage bag over it and cut a small hole for the fermentation lock. (My friend Tom Ayres covers *his* carboys with T-shirts.)

Siphon hose, spigot, and filler.   Because of the yeast sediment in both primary and secondary fermentation, you can't just pour the beer from one vessel to another through a funnel. Instead, you need four to five feet of clear plastic tubing with an inside diameter of about three-eighths of an inch to siphon it off with a minimum of agitation. Into *what* vessel is still debated in our household. Should it be the eight-gallon boiling pot or the four-gallon mashing pot? Usually it's the latter, and I transfer the last of the beer from the fermenter without priming sugar.

When I started brewing, in the Dark Ages before home brew was legal, the only way I could control the flow of wort into the bottles was to pinch the end of the tubing. I never got the tube completely closed, and I would spill three or four bottles' worth during each session. Then plastic crimpers arrived. They worked, but they were brittle and often broke. Along came plastic stopcocks, which fit snugly on the end of the tube. They required two hands but they didn't leak, break, or otherwise let you down. Next came Phil's Philler, a brass device which uses gravity to fill bottles cleanly and expeditiously. I'm a convert. (Now, if you have lots of discretionary income, there is even a miniature professional counter-flow bottler for the home brewer.)

Brushes.   Almost every home brewing text recommends a bottle brush. I don't know why. If a bottle is so scuzzy or scummy that you need a brush to clean it, you shouldn't reuse it. However, a twelve-to-eighteen-inch flexible brush is very helpful in cleaning a carboy, especially around the neck, where bits of hops and proteins adhere and dry. (The best cleanser is trisodium phosphate, the active ingredient in dishwasher detergents.)

Bottles.   In my early brewing days, I didn't care about the size of the bottles. I took what was available, a potpourri of squat LaBatt's, standard Budweiser bar bottles, Piels pints, porcelain-capped Grolsch flagons, twenty-two-ounce Tooth's Sheaf Stout bottles, and Narragansett quarts. Meanwhile, I collected over eighty bottles from thirty foreign countries and the United States, and these ringed our kitchen cabinets like the Parthenon's frieze.

As time went by, and bottles lost their aesthetic appeal and bottling its therapeutic benefit, I looked for ways to speed up the process. A friend told me American champagne bottles would take a crown cap. What's more, a local motel was pushing champagne breakfasts. The innkeeper was a member of our church, so I asked him if I could come collect his empties. He laughed and said sure, it would cut down on his trash bill. In a trice, I cut my bottling time by a third. Champagne bottles hold just over twenty-five ounces, so a five-gallon batch required only twenty-four instead of forty-eight to fifty-four bottles.

In the last few years, I have switched to Grolsch bottles exclusively. Since Vermont has a container deposit law, most bottles and cans are returned to grocery stores or beverage centers. I've usually "bought" these bottles for from 10 to 20 cents each, or borrowed them from a friend who no longer brews. The sixteen-ounce size is appropriate when I have one beer on a weekday night. What's more important, capping is a breeze, and rubber washers are readily available.

Caution: Don't use no-return bottles, because the glass is not strong enough to hold well-primed home brew. Finally, don't use those bottles with twist-off caps; the brewery can get a tight seal, but you won't.

Capper.   There are several on the market, including one bizarre style that requires a hammer. I still have the same bench capper I bought twenty years ago for $6. Mine has capped over eight thousand bottles without a miss. Today, these cappers cost from $12 to $35, depending upon whether they have one handle or two. If you use different-sized bottles, make sure your capper can adjust its height.

Always fill bottles to within an inch or an inch and a half from the top. Never cap half-full bottles. Contrary to common sense, these build up far greater pressure than those with less head space.

Sanitation.   One can't discuss bottles, or bottling, or brewing, without considering cleanliness. The three cardinal rules of good brewing, according to Michael Lewis, are "sanitation, sanitation, and sanitation."

I have gone through a metamorphosis in my own cleaning technique. At one point, I was washing bottles with water, rinsing with a bleach solution, then rerinsing with sodium metabisulphite and again with water. The tedium of filling the bottles was a lark compared with the cleaning. Then I took Fred Eckhardt's advice: sterilize everything with a chlorine solution and drip-dry. I now make a solution of sterilant with one tablespoon of chlorine bleach per gallon of water. Bottles get a fifteen-to-twenty-minute soak. All other tools of the trade—tubing, spoons, fermenters, etc.—get a soak, too, until ready for use. Then I give them a quick rinse with tap water, except for the plastic tube, which receives a shot of boiling-hot water.

Always wash out bottles promptly after drinking the beer. The residual yeast is both a home to bacteria and, when hardened, nearly as tough to remove as plaque from your teeth.

Thermometer. In making extract beers, a thermometer's chief uses are in helping you find the right temperature for adding yeast and in letting you know how much to adjust the hydrometer's reading as the wort temperature diverges from 60° F. Thermometers are vital in mashing, for the brewer must take accurate readings between 120° and 180° F. Candy or dairy thermometers fill this bill.

Strainer. Needed to collect grains or whole hops after a boil. A stainless-steel colander, layers of cheesecloth, or specially made filter bags are suitable. They should be sanitized first.

Spoon. This implement should be at least twelve inches long. Stainless steel is easier to clean, plastic is cheap, and wood "feels" the best. ("Buffalo Bill" Owens uses a canoe paddle in his brewpub.)

Funnel. Helpful for pouring liquids such as wort or yeast starters into the small opening of a carboy.

Pots and pans. Varying sizes for preparing priming sugars, gelatin, gypsum, and small amounts of hot water for rinsing things like siphon tubes.

Scale. Essential for weighing small batches of hops and specialty grains. The small postal variety works well.

Brewing journal. For the scientist, taking detailed, careful notes is essential to successful experimentation and replication. The social scientists can quote philosopher George Santayana: "Those who cannot remember the past are condemned to repeat it." When I look back at my notes for my first score of batches, I am appalled at their skimpiness. Beyond a mere recitation of ingredients, there is nothing, no comments, no evaluation, nothing upon which I could draw for improvements. With such scanty records, I was not much better off than the prehistoric shaman who saw brewing as magic beyond his control.

In *your* journal you should note the ingredients, procedure, any special circumstances, and the results, especially any failures. Nothing is more certain than human readiness to forget a mistake and its causes. My mind usually does not register lapses into sloth, cussedness, distraction, or errors of judgment, unless I write down what I did in the first place. *Good records produce good beer.*

ALL-GRAIN EQUIPMENT

When I began brewing there were few all-grain brewers, because good ingredients were hard to obtain and most brewers had to fabricate all their own equipment and it took all day to brew a batch. It still takes most of a day to brew an all-grain batch, but the vast improvement in equipment has paralleled the explosion in available ingredients. Between 10 and 20 percent of American home brewers are now making all-grain beers. Most all-grain brewers have some technically experimental bent. They like prowling around junkyards. They are not daunted by stainless-steel welding. They like pumps and tubing.

I think that the main reason more people don't brew all-grain is TIME. It does take most of a day to mash and boil an all-grain batch. Furthermore, such brewing requires more elaborate and expensive equipment. You, the brewer, must set your own priorities. The all-grain brewer crows about the beer's flavor and uniqueness, not about its cost.

Grinders and mills.   Only a handful of home brewers malt their own grain. All-grain brewing, therefore, begins with malted grains, usually barleys. Home brewing shops will usually grind grain for a slight fee, but most home brewers want to do it themselves.

Knowing how to grind the grain is at least as important as finding the machinery to do it. Food processors and coffee grinders produce too fine a powder and take too long. A blender makes the grain too coarse.

The kernels must be ground just enough to crack open the husks and expose the starchy innards. During mashing, this starch is liquefied and removed from the husks. During sparging, the husks form a filter bed through which the sugary liquor drains, leaving the husks behind.

Today, the home brewer has two major choices: grinders or roller mills. Fifteen years ago, I bought a hand-powered Corona grinder for about $30, and I use it still. It takes about one minute to grind one pound of malt. I rather enjoy those ten to twelve minutes of grinding. I feel at one with the overworked and underappreciated camels and cattle of Mesopotamia and Egypt which turned millstones for beermakers millennia ago. But there are other brewers less patient than I. They have hooked up small electric motors to their grinders.

The second option is to buy a roller mill, for $80–110. This device (which also can be electrified) is quicker and more efficient than the grinder. Again, you need to decide whether the extra $50–80 is worth it.

Mashing vessel. A five-gallon batch of all-grain beer contains between eight and twelve pounds of grain. This must be mashed at a ratio of about one quart of water per pound of grain. Since you will need to stir the mash a good deal, you want a vessel of three-and-a-half-to-five-gallon capacity. I have used the same stainless-steel soup kettle for fifteen years and will probably keep it for another fifteen, if I don't move up to ten-gallon batches.

pH papers and meters. These are useful for measuring the acidity of the mashing water. The scale, between 4.8 and 7.0, is tricky to read if you, like me, are red-green color-blind. But with some practice you can get approximate readings. For the technocrats, there are now digital meters for measuring pH. They cost $40 or more.

Sparging equipment. I spent more time experimenting with this stage of brewing than with all others combined. It may have been my mechanical ineptitude; or it may have been the lack of knowledgeable texts or friends.

Sparging occurs after the malt enzymes have done their best to convert the starches to fermentable sugars. The aim is to rinse the sugars out of the grain while leaving behind as much haze-forming proteins and husks as possible. My system consists of two food-grade plastic buckets, such as health food stores use for tofu (but not for any kind of oil), or doughnut shops for jelly. One should hold four gallons and the other six gallons. About an inch above the bottom of the larger bucket, I drill a hole and insert a plastic spigot such as you see on coffee urns. These are available from restaurant supply stores. Next, I drill about two hundred three-sixteenths-of-an-inch holes in the bottom of the smaller bucket. This bucket slips snugly inside the larger one and rests about three inches off the bottom, because the rim holds it at this level. The sugar-laden water can now pass through while the false bottom collects the grain husks.

Another common sparging setup advocated by brewpub guru Bill Owens and by Paul Hale is the standard camp cooler. Paul cuts six feet of half-inch copper tubing into sections. With a hacksaw he cuts parallel slices in the tubing every half-inch. He caps one end of each section and joins the other to a union at the other end, which is connected to an exit pipe.*

Sparge water vessel.   For a five-gallon batch of beer, you need about six gallons of sparging water at about 170° F. Sparging takes between fifteen and thirty minutes, and the water should not drop much below 160° during this time. I have used a five-gallon canning pot, a three-gallon soup pot, and an English device called a Bruheater to give me that supply of sparging water.

Wort chiller.   Like a football receiver fully extended to catch a pass, home brew is at its most vulnerable between the end of the boil and the time the yeast has begun its magical work in a closed fermenter. If you wait for hot wort to cool down by itself, it can take twelve to twenty hours. Even if you leave the vessel outside in 20° F. weather in Vermont, it still takes six to eight hours. Immersing the vessel in cold water cuts the time to two hours, but manhandling fifty pounds of hot liquid is no joy. Enter the heat exchanger. There are two types here: counter-flow and immersion.

---

* For a complete description, see Bill Owens's excellent booklet *How to Build a Small Brewery,* $5.00 (Box 510, Hayward, CA 94541-0510).

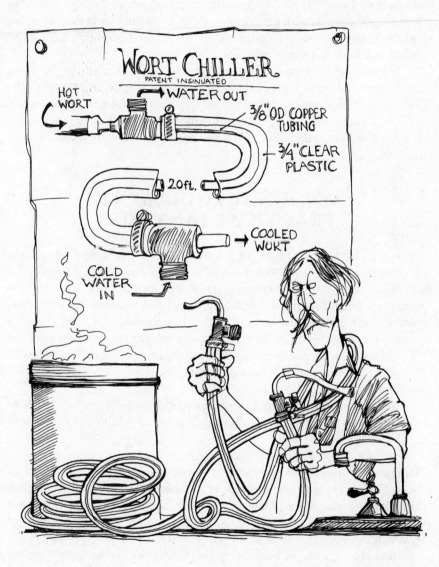

One of the first people to make and sell the counter-flow system was Al Andrews, an avid home brewer from Riverside, California. It consisted of about twenty feet of copper tubing inside an equivalent length of clear plastic tubing, with appropriate fittings. The hot wort runs one way and tap water the other ("counter-flow") and a five-gallon batch can be cooled in fifteen to twenty minutes.

The immersion type is a coil of copper which is attached to the water tap. By circulating tap water through the tube, you draw heat from the hot wort and reach yeast "pitching" temperature in about thirty minutes.

The counter-flow system is more efficient—i.e., it takes less time to cool the wort—but it is harder to clean. You have to decide which is more important.

OPTIONAL EQUIPMENT, PRACTICAL FANTASIES

The search for better equipment is a trail of broken promises—the same promise: "If I can only get this valve [or keg, or mash tun, or cooker], I will be content." For most brewers it doesn't work out that way. The all-grain equipment fever of acquisition is rather like malaria: once you contract it, you never quite get rid of it, though you can keep it under control. On the other hand, brewers are not solely to blame. Temptations abound today where few existed ten to twelve years ago. The pages of *Zymurgy* are filled with ads for equipment, including complete stainless-steel brewing systems.

With the caveat that my term *optional* can transform itself into *necessary* before my very eyes, I offer a selection of additional equipment below.

Bruheater.   Unlike the wort chiller, which moved from "fantasy" to "necessity" overnight, the Bruheater remained optional. This English invention is a six-gallon plastic vessel with its own heating element and rheostat for controlling temperature. Its makers proclaim its wide usage for mashing, boiling, and heating sparge water. It costs $80 or more, not counting the expense of converting the English outlet to a three-prong 220-volt plug. The problems were two: one, it took a long time to raise the wort or mash temperature; two, without constant stirring, you risk burning some of the mash on the heating coil. Consequently, I limited my use to heating sparging water.

Propane stoves. These come under a variety of trade names. As more brewers move out of the kitchen (and off the stove) and into the basement, more are converting to these convenient devices, which deliver 15,000 to 30,000 BTU's to the bottom of boiling vessels. Using this simple stove, I can mash and boil conveniently. For example, I can take wort from 160° to 212° F. in about fifteen minutes. Such devices are imperative if one is brewing more than five-gallon batches.

Bottle washer. This device, which fits over a water spigot and has a pressure-release action, sprays the inside of bottles with tap water. It costs between $10 and $13. If I have picked up bottles from an outside source, I first soak a bottle in my chlorine bleach solution (one tablespoon per gallon) for ten to fifteen minutes. (Never use soap or detergents to clean bottles, because they wreak havoc with the beer's head.) Then I rinse them with the bottle washer.

Kegs. No matter how much you love bringing out a bottle of beer, or shagging your brew over to friends, there comes a time when you grow weary of cleaning and filling hundreds of bottles. You are ready to keg. Kegs turn your basement into a pub, where your thirsty legs can carry you to tap a glass or a pitcher with the flick of a finger.

I began my search at Burlington's only junkyard and luckily found six 7.75-gallon Narragansett quarter-barrels at scrap metal prices—$10 apiece. I bought three. Cleaning was first. With caustic soda I bummed from the local milk plant, I cleaned them as best I could.

Enter St. Gambrinus, the patron saint of brewing, to reward me for a good deed. One morning I called up the city streets department to compliment them for rapidly sanding an icy patch of roadway. I got into a conversation with Bill Rockwell, the assistant superintendent. He brought up home brewing, because he was a brewer and he had read of our attempt to mount a brewing contest at the county fair. One thing led to another, and it turned out he and a friend in the parks department had already kegged half a dozen batches. They'd used the same size kegs. They filled

them with three-quarters of a ten-gallon batch and bottled the rest. What's more, Rockwell had a CO_2 dispenser that allowed him to drink the beer from the keg for three or four weeks without its going flat.

Rockwell said his only disaster had occurred when he had a ten-gallon batch ready to transfer out of the fermenter into the keg. Thinking he could watch some baseball during this process, he forgot to check on the system. Somehow one end of the siphon hose flipped out of the keg, and seven of the ten gallons formed a lake in the kitchen before obeying the law of gravity to end up in the basement. It was days before he got it all cleaned up.

To fill my first keg, I simply mixed seven and a half gallons from a light and a dark ale I had aging in carboys. I found a wooden bung in a hardware store, boiled it for five minutes, and pounded it home with a four-pound sledgehammer. Over the hot summer, the keg sat in our 60° F. basement until, at the end of August, we tapped it for the christening of our first son. I rented a simple hand pump tapper system from the beverage store. Toward the end of the afternoon, as the natural CO_2 dissipated, the beer went a little flat, but its taste remained first-rate and we drank it to the lees.

Tapping and drinking an entire keg at one time is okay, but fleeting. Why not home brew on tap? That meant buying a CO_2 pressure system. Chris made that my next Christmas present, thus saving me the agony of justifying a $150 purchase. This system worked well for several years. What pleasure, what ease, to trip to the basement and return with a pitcher of cool foamy lager or ale.

This system had two drawbacks. First, I had to make ten-gallon batches. The second was the difficulty of chilling one of those squat kegs. I solved the first problem when I discovered five-gallon Cornelius kegs (like those used for dispensing soft drinks). I went back to five-gallon batches happily. The second I solved with a . . .

Spare refrigerator.   With this appliance I could kill two birds with one stone. I could maintain lagers at a proper temperature (Al Andrews kept four Cornelius kegs in his refrigerator simultaneously, with a four-spigot tapper system jutting out of the door). I could also do proper "lagering," which means holding lagers at temperatures in the low-30's F. range. That addition to my equipment improved my lagers by 100 percent.

Ever more advanced brewing.   Just by perusing the pages of *Zymurgy*, one can see new products in every issue—yeast culturing kits, complete brewhouses in stainless steel, elaborate roller mills, etc. Further, every issue has readers' suggestions for equipment improvements. In particular, I suggest consulting the Special Issue of *Zymurgy*, Vol. 15, No. 4: "Gadgets and Equipment." As more and more home brewers improve their skills and processes, they will soon be bumping up against professional equipment and complexity. Suppliers now see profit in making "pilot" brewing systems for the home brewer. Some of these cost over $1,000.

Of course, you don't have to be an engineer to brew your own beer. But it helps to have an innovative bent, an inquiring streak, and a resolve to improve. I love the American Homebrewers Association dearly, for they have done more to promote good beer and good brewing in this country than any other organization. But their motto bothers me: "Relax. Don't Worry. Have a Homebrew." When I am making beer, especially all-grain beer, I cannot afford to relax until the yeast has been pitched. Making beer is serious business. I would modify the motto to the less catchy, but (for me) more appropriate: "Pay attention. Worry intelligently. And have a homebrew when you're done."

One final caveat. The secret to making good beer is to worry about those factors which will improve it. As Michael Lewis has said: "It is all very well to enthuse over Saaz hops or a fancy CO_2 system, but unless you pay attention to sanitation, your beer will be bad. Sanitation is dull; but scrupulous, resolute, obsessive attention to cleanliness is far more important for good beer than all the fancy ingredients and equipment you may assemble."

All-Grain Brewing

All of what follows involves a five-gallon batch, since most home brewers work with this volume. My "dream" lager is the incomparable Pilsner Urquell. My grandparents emigrated to Montana from a Bohemian town one hundred miles east of Pilsen. I call this emulation Ma Vlast *(My Fatherland) Lager to honor my Czech heritage. The recipe is a variation of one I found in Dave Miller's book* The Complete Handbook of Home Brewing.

I begin with the yeast. Unless you plan to use the lees from a previous batch to launch your beer, you need to build a yeast starter before you begin to brew. This is because most yeast packets, dry or liquid, don't have enough oomph to start a lively fermentation. Unless I have a batch in hand, or have bummed some yeast from local brewer Greg Noonan, I brew with liquid yeasts. Twenty-four to thirty-six hours before brewing begins, I start the fermentation in the prepared pack. On the night before brewing, I prepare a weak wort with four or five tablespoons of dried malt extract boiled in a pint of water. I let that cool, then add the yeast, cover, and let it build up so that, if my timing is good, it will be ready to "pitch" just as I finish my brewing cycle. Of course, my timing is not always perfect; no big deal. What matters is that the yeast now has a running start to get fermentation under way in that vulnerable time.

Brewing day begins with a hot cup of coffee. That's because it is 5:00 a.m. and I need to be wide awake when I enter my basement-brewery.

Awaiting me there is ten pounds of six-row barley I ground the night before, about ten minutes' work.

I fire up my propane stove to heat ten quarts of water to 135° F. (one quart per pound of grain) in my four-gallon stainless-steel pot. I know from asking the city water department that the tap water has a neutral pH of 7.1 with medium hardness (120 parts per million of carbonates) and no sulphates. For this pale lager, I want a pH of 5.6, so I add three teaspoons of gypsum (calcium sulphate)—two teaspoons to the mash water, and one to be held for the sparging water. The calcium sulphate reacts with the phosphorus in the malt to produce a weak phosphorous acid, which lowers the pH. Such acidity is necessary for efficient mashing, good protein "breaks," and proper coagulation of solids for a clear beer.

Next I pour the ground grain into the mash water, stirring well with a long-handled spoon to break up any clumps. The temperature should fall to 120° to 122° F. and the mash be the consistency of half-cooked oatmeal. The "protein rest" occurs between 118° and 122° and lasts between thirty and forty minutes. Such a "rest" is necessary to break down the proteins, so that later in the brewing process they will settle out and not cause residual haze in the beer.

(Sometimes I will brew and bottle on the same day, and I use blocks of time like this forty-five minutes to clean bottles.)

The next step is to raise the mash temperature to between 150° and 158° F., to convert the starches. I accomplish this in one of two ways. I may simply turn up the propane heater, a process which requires constant stirring to avoid scorching the mash. Or I follow my friend Paul Hale's advice and add measured amounts of boiling water to the mash—although I don't use the camp cooler mash tun (described on page 82) that Paul swears by, because the boiling-water technique works fine in my stainless-steel mash tun. Paul says the advantages of his system are: no scorching; and, because the cooler is so well insulated, no drop in temperature.*

Once conversion is complete, it is time to kill off the enzymes. If I don't do this, I will end up with too thin a beer, because all of the body-building dextrins will convert to maltose and subsequently be fermented. The executioner is more heat. I bring the temperature up to 168° F.,

---

* For an excellent description of this technique, see Bill Owens, *How to Build a Small Brewery.*

stirring all the while. This stabilizes the ratio between maltose and dextrins in the beer.

(At the risk of being pedantic, I remind you to write down what you do at each step, so that you will know what changes, if any, you want to make with your next batch.)

During the second stage of mashing, I prepare six gallons of sparging water at 170° F. This may take some juggling of pots and vessels. Formerly, I used a Bruheater (see page 84). Now I use the propane stove. Remember that sparging will take twenty to thirty minutes and the water should remain around 170° F. for effective rinsing of the grains.

Now comes the part of brewing that used to give me ulcers. I put the vessel with my sparging water on top of the clothes drier. Below it, on a sturdy stool, sit my mashing buckets, one inside the other. On the floor is my stainless-steel mash tun for collecting the wort.

First I fill the space between the bottom of the outer bucket and the many-holed bottom of the inner bucket with about half a gallon of 175° F. water. This is to prevent a vacuum from forming as I draw off the first runnings. Then I ladle the grainy "goods" into the inner bucket. I pour in just enough extra hot water to cover the top of the grain. I let this stand for five minutes.

The reason for "underletting" the grains with water is explained by Professor Michael Lewis: "You have a bunch of particles that are suspended in the wort you have produced. The particles are exhausted and the one thing you must not do is compact the bed. Don't begin the runoff right away. When you do, slide the wort *out* from among the particles and slide the sparge water *in* from the top. In other words, as you drain out the wort from the bottom, you add sparging water from the top. Gradually, you sneak up on the particles, replacing the wort in which they are suspended with hot water. If you draw out the wort too quickly, the bed will collapse and you will have a stuck mash."

A stuck mash is a brewer's nightmare. It is like letting wallpaper paste set too long. It means you must dredge up all the "goods" and start the mash over again. This is a messy, time-consuming process that will affect the final maltose-dextrin ratio, probably give you a weaker final beer, and seriously deplete your good humor.

To transport the sparge water, I run it through a cane-shaped copper-tube/plastic-tube device with a stopcock. I start running the water slowly. Then, from the stopcock at the bottom of the mash tun, I draw off a quart or so of the first cloudy runnings. Gently, I pour that back onto the top of the grain bed, draw off another quart, and repeat the process. Then I open the tap and let it drain into the collecting vessel on the floor. I match the inflow from the hot-water vessel to the outflow from the mash tun's bottom. I want to keep the water level just above the level of the grains. One can't rush this process. I find that I can do other basement chores while the sparging proceeds, as long as I watch the water level.

When I have three gallons of wort, I pour them into my eight-gallon boiling vessel on the propane stove and turn on the heat. I continue the sparging until I have another three gallons, which then goes into the boiling vessel. (That is a total of six gallons for a five-gallon batch, because I expect to lose two to three quarts in steam.) While the wort is heating up (and filling the basement with the sweet redolence of malt), I carry the spent grains out to the compost for next year's carrots and tomatoes.

A watched pot *will* boil—more important, it *won't* boil over. To clean up after a boil-over is to swear off inattention forever. Yet you need a good, rolling, kicking boil before you can add any hops. This period is called the "hot break," when malt proteins begin to coagulate into larger and larger clumps. It is one of the most dramatic (and at first sight unsettling) phenomena in brewing. The proteins gather like storm clouds against a gray-green sky. The first time I saw this, I was convinced I had done something wrong and I dumped the batch.

After thirty minutes of boiling, I add an ounce of bittering hops. The variety doesn't matter as long as the alpha acid content is medium—5–7 percent. You must stand there and control the burner to guard against a possible boil-over. When the froth recedes, you can adjust the heat to give a controlled, rolling boil. (During the boil, two marriages take place—one unites the bitter hops with the sweet malt; the other joins the hops' tannins with malt proteins to form additional clumps which will eventually sink of their own weight.) Thirty minutes later, I add another half an ounce of the same hops. I also throw in a teaspoon of Irish Moss to help clear the beer.

After ninety minutes, I turn off the heat, wait five minutes, and put in my aromatic hops. For this imitation Pilsner Urquell, I use one-half to three-quarters of an ounce of Saaz pellets, which produces the enduring flavor of this style of beer. For this (and for all beers) the aromatic hops should be the freshest and most flavorful.

After you have let the wort rest for half an hour, it is time to transfer the wort to the fermenter. If for some reason I have used loose hops, it is necessary to strain them out so that they don't clog the take-up tube in the next stage. I pour the wort through a sanitized fine-mesh plastic cloth. Some brewers worry a lot about the suspended proteinous material, or *trub*, that precipitates out. I don't, as long as it doesn't block my take-up tube.

Now it's time to chill the wort. This is important for two reasons. One, you want to get the yeast working as quickly as possible, because the wort is most vulnerable to infection at these temperatures. Two, this so-called cold break also helps to coagulate the proteinous materials and thereby clear the future beer. I use an immersion-type wort chiller. This coil of copper tubing connects to the water faucet at one end and to another spigot at the other. The cool tap water flows through it and cools the surrounding wort to yeast pitching temperature. It is a bit slower than the counter-flow technique, where the beer flows through a copper tube inside a water-filled garden hose. However, it is much easier to sanitize, because it is immersed in 200° F. wort.

Either way is much faster than my former system of immersing one stainless-steel pot in the other, and changing the surrounding water several times.

Once the wort is chilled, I transfer it to the fermenter. To start the liquid transfer, I fill a sanitized plastic tube with hot water, insert one end in the brew kettle, and cover the other end with my (sanitized) finger. With the fermenter lower than the brew kettle, I release the latter end. The water flows out, drawing the wort down the tube. As soon as it reaches the end, I direct the flow into the fermenter. Why jump through these hoops? To avoid the millions of germs in my mouth if I should suck the wort, not to mention scalding myself.

Halfway through the transfer, I add the yeast starter. When the carboy is almost full, I draw off just enough wort to fill my hydrometer tube, so that I know my original gravity (and therefore my *potential* alcohol content).

When the carboy is filled, I add my yeast starter, give the vessel a good shaking, and then insert one end of a sanitized plastic blow-by (or blow-out) tube into the neck of the carboy. (The reason for this rousing is that the yeast needs oxygen to begin multiplying. Later on, ambient air becomes an enemy, because of the bacteria it carries, but at this moment it is a friend.) The other end goes into a bucket with about one gallon of sterilant (one tablespoon of chlorine per gallon of water).

You may choose to do all your fermentation in one vessel. The great advantage is that contamination is almost impossible if the beer is not transferred. Further, some of the froth and foam of the early fermentation may be pushed up and out the tube, or at least cling to the carboy walls.

Within four to twelve hours, depending upon the yeast variety, the surface shows fermentation activity. Foam gathers on the surface, bringing brownish protein and hops particles with it to form a dark froth like dirty whipping cream.

In twenty-four hours, fermentation should be in full cry. (But don't panic if it is not. Yeasts vary widely in their activity. And if you have pitched the yeast from a packet, the process will certainly take longer than with a yeast starter.) By the end of the third day, the first bloom has subsided. If I have filled the carboy to the top, one to two quarts of wort may have blown out. (Lagers don't foam as much as ales.)

Where I have used the lees of a previous batch, fermentation may begin within an hour. I remember once putting the carboy in the bathroom rather than the basement (which was 20° cooler) and returning thirty minutes later to find foam pushing through the blow-by tube.

After primary fermentation subsides, I transfer the beer to a second, sanitized fermenter, leaving the trub in the primary fermenter. Secondary fermentation lasts about two weeks. I let the beer ferment flat. My rule of thumb is to wait until the frequency of bubbles has slowed to one every ninety seconds or longer.

Now comes the stage from which comes the beer style's name. *Lagern* in German means to "store." Lagering helps to clear the beer visually and to absorb some of the off-flavors spawned at higher temperatures. I will store this beer in a keg (or in bottles) at 33–34° F. for a month in my spare refrigerator.

I confess to some inconsistency in my priming technique. Sometimes I will prime the beer with a half-cup of dried malt extract boiled in a pint of water before kegging (or bottling). And sometimes I will just let the beer naturally "condition" in those vessels.

Before I bought the extra refrigerator, I made acceptable lager by keeping the bottles under 60° F., but with proper refrigeration the beer was distinctly better, whether in keg or bottle.

Unquestionably, lager requires more deferred gratification than ale. Lagering should last four to six weeks. That's okay with me, because in the interim I have other batches of beer in different stages of aging. I don't expect that anyone who has taken on this elaborate process is an utter neophyte.

There is no way of avoiding the seven or eight hours of brewing time in making lagers. I weave other chores and basement clean-up into the process, so it doesn't appear like some temporal black hole in the week. Lately, I have been making lagers almost exclusively.

For me, a marathon runner, lagers are the "Boston" of beers. That is, you need to qualify in a certain time; at my age now, that's three hours and thirty minutes. Training for and running a marathon takes preparation and persistence. But then, unless you are sick, you will finish. Making the "cut," however, demands extra effort. So do lagers. When I make successful lagers, I have conquered the technical, biological, and aesthetic complexities of the dominant beer style in this country. I have beaten Busch and Miller and Stroh's.*

With lagers there is no place to hide, and when I have made good lagers, there is no *reason* to hide. I am king of the brewery!

* For an exhaustive treatment of lager brewing, see Greg Noonan's *Brewing Lager Beer*.

A Busman's Holiday

One fall afternoon, the postman brought the usual load of political appeals, junk mail, three newspapers, and a few pieces of legitimate first-class mail. Almost lost among the flashy catalogues for tools and kitchenware was a brown package from Chris's sister, who was then studying in England. Inside was a paperback book entitled *The Good Beer Guide* published by the Campaign for Real Ale (CAMRA).

In language reminiscent of a nineteenth-century broadside, the *Guide* began:

> Ladies and Gentlemen of the Drinking Public. Once again the Campaign for Real Ale presents for your delectation almost 6,000 of the very Finest Hostelries in these Islands that dispense that great delight: Traditional Draft Beer. Members of the Campaign have spared no effort to seek out Sundry Inns, Taverns and Public Houses that keep and serve their Ale in the most Excellent of Condition.

Traditional draft beer or ale, the jacket cover continued, is brewed only from malted barley, water, hops, and yeast to make the bitters, milds, and porters. The means of dispensing are several—from the cask, the beer engine, or electric power—"but all these Systems eschew the Noisome Carbonic Gas which the Purveyors of Inferior Brew use to mask the Lackluster Taste of their Dubious Products."

Here were words to warm the heart of all brewing purists. I spent the evening with a pint of home-brewed porter, perusing the *Guide* as dreamily as a dedicated pub crawler might examine a map of London. The *Guide* gave a brief history of the venerable English pub, telling how that institution was the outgrowth of hearty private hospitality. It also listed all of the nation's 170 operating breweries along with their addresses and telephone numbers.

Both Chris and I had been to England several times, and she had lived there for seven years—albeit before she reached drinking age. We liked the hearty English ales and stouts. Four years earlier, we had driven around southern Ireland and in twelve days managed to explore some forty-four bars and the bottoms of countless glasses of Guinness, Murphy's, and Smithwick's Ale. We were experienced, if not hardened, pub crawlers.

Why not make a vacation of visiting some of these small breweries listed in the CAMRA *Guide?* I had toured two breweries in this country, the Anheuser Busch plant in Merrimack, New Hampshire (capacity 3 million barrels a year), and the world's largest brewery, Coors, in Golden, Colorado (15 million barrels). These were not breweries, they were factories—as impersonal and sterile and remote from good beer as giant bakeries are from homemade bread. The CAMRA *Guide* described small breweries producing as little as a hundred gallons per week.

We had friends in Oxfordshire who would find us a place to stay, and a quick look at the *Guide* revealed seven breweries within thirty miles of Stonesfield, our prospective base. We contacted our friends and dispatched letters to those seven breweries, asking if we could tour their establishments. We didn't expect any replies; we only hoped they would be hospitable when we arrived.

Before describing the breweries we visited, I should say something about the origins of CAMRA and English home brewing.

Imagine thousands of outraged housewives turned loose on Procter & Gamble and Lever Brothers, demanding that they make "real" soap. Imagine American beer drinkers picketing Schlitz to change the formulation of its beer. Imagine other beer lovers filing a friend-of-the-court brief against General Brewing Company's takeover of Pearl Brewing Co. With only modest exaggeration, this gives some idea of what beer historian Michael Jackson calls "the most successful consumer movement in history."

The spiritual ancestor of CAMRA was a beer-drinking club in Britain called The Society for the Preservation of Beers from the Wood. This became the Campaign for the Revitalization of Ale and subsequently, in 1973, the present Campaign for Real Ale. The cause attracted a hodge-podge of beer lovers, food nuts, defenders of the English pub, traditionalists, small-is-beautiful advocates, and home brewers. Within five years, the Campaign had 20,000 members in 140 local chapters across Great Britain. Its members came from all socioeconomic classes, but the largest and most vociferous group consisted of young professionals.

CAMRA members united to fight twin devils: "concentration and pressurization." They claimed that traditional, living, cask-conditioned ale was being progressively destroyed by the business and brewing tactics of the so-called Big Six major brewing companies: Courage, Allied Breweries, Scottish & Newcastle, Watneys, Bass Charrington, and Whitbread. By 1970, the Big Six were producing over 80 percent of all the beer sold in Britain. Their relentless drive for economies of scale dictated that they sell fewer varieties to more people. This they did by building ever-larger "mega-keggeries" and shipping the beer by huge lorries throughout the country. The Big Six also followed the pattern of giant American breweries in formulating their brews for the lowest common denominator of taste.

A CAMRA member compared the mass-produced "keg beer" with "real ale" and found, "It is essentially the difference between real draft beer, a living product in which fermentation continues in the pub cellar, and filtered beer, which is sterile (all living yeast organisms having been removed) and which needs added carbon dioxide in order to recreate the 'lively' appearance of draft beer."

Not only were the Big Six pasteurizing and homogenizing ales, as their American cousins were doing, they were also introducing Continental-style lagers into their pubs. And this lighter, clearer, colder beverage was picking up an increasing market share. To the purists it was as if baseball had begun to cut into cricket's popularity. By the early 1980s, lager's market share was over 20 percent and climbing strongly.

The Big Six did not flourish simply by building larger beer factories. They acquired scores of small breweries and either shut them down or turned them to the production of Big Six brands. The effect of these buyouts on customer choice was particularly stifling because of the British system of "tied-houses." Since the eighteenth century, most of the pubs in Britain have been owned by breweries. By 1980, over 80 percent of the pubs—that is, 60,000—were operated by the Big Six. Once they possessed these outlets, the breweries were naturally disinclined to sell beers other than their own.

From CAMRA's standpoint, an even worse sin occurred when a member of the Big Six bought and closed a smaller regional brewery and shut down the attached pubs as well. In hundreds of cases, this left villages without a center. As the president of one small brewery said, "A village that loses its pub starts to die. I would never want to be responsible for administering that kind of blow."

As an example of what could happen, Courage acquired a Bristol brewery in 1961. Between its own pubs and those of the formerly independent company, Courage suddenly controlled 64 percent of the drinking places in the city of Avon. An American might not care if Budweiser sold 64 percent of the beer in his town, but the English CAMRA members regarded it as a tragedy and an outrage.

They were convinced that, if unchecked, the industry concentration would eliminate all the real draft beer in the country. So they set themselves to patronizing and defending those smaller regional breweries that still made real ale. In addition, they filed a number of studies and reports with the government Price and Food Standards Commissions to show that smaller breweries offered better value, and castigated the Big Six for failing to offer information about their ingredients. As they marched to protest the closing of small breweries, they picked up reams of national publicity.

By the mid-1970s, to everyone's surprise, the Big Six were on the defensive. The Monopolies Commission took a more careful look at their takeover proposals. Several of the Big Six resurrected the names, if not the formulations, of breweries they had swallowed. What's more, they spent millions of pounds proclaiming their devotion to "real ale."

At about the same time, and no doubt spurred by CAMRA's success, a score of small breweries opened up, among them the first new brewery in London in fifty years. One traditional brewer said that the survival of many small regional beermakers might not have been possible without the support of the CAMRA movement.

Interestingly, a comparative study in Britain found that the local and regional breweries were significantly more profitable than the Big Six, as long as they kept to the area they could best supply and serve. The majors were simply spread too thin. A significant factor in the success of small brewers was their production of "real ale."

Modern English home brewing dates from 1963, when Chancellor of the Exchequer Reginald Maudling lifted all restrictions on private brewing, provided none was sold. In a curious parallel to the American experience, British home brewing had been declining almost to oblivion since 1880. The reasons for it were quite different, however. In America, local breweries sprang up in so many communities that there was little aesthetic or financial incentive to compete at home. In Britain, however, many people brewed for distinctly economic reasons, and in 1880 the Gladstone government imposed a tax that made it cheaper for the poor (for whose benefit the tax was supposedly levied) to buy beer from the "common," or public, brewers than to make their own.

Home brewing grew rapidly in the 1960s under a combination of influences: rebellion against pasteurized keg beer, reduced choice in commercial beer, increase in leisure time, and the rising cost of beer in pubs, where 80 percent of British brews are consumed. Lacking good information and equipment, many home brewers weighed in heavily with the sugar. The resulting beers were cannon fodder for the cartoonists and wags of the day.

As the decade progressed, home brewers refined their taste and the malting companies responded with improved malts and hops. The companies began to produce kits with premixed hops and malt. Just add water, boil, cool, add yeast, and away you go. So popular were the kits that the nation's largest drugstore chain, Boots, became the largest retailer of home brewing supplies, garnering millions of pounds in sales per year. By 1980, an estimated 10 percent of the beer consumed in England was being made at home.

In England, a pint of beer in a pub is five to seven times more expensive than one brewed at home. No matter how much a fellow wants to hang out at his friendly "local," if he has limited funds and an unlimited thirst, he will inevitably turn to home brewing. By contrast, the cost differential between commercial American beer and decent home brew is closer to 2:1. British kits are convenient, simple, consistent, and . . .

boring. English home brew supply shops offer a range of malts, hops, and yeasts, but the vast majority of their customers buy the same ingredients month-in and month-out, because they brew for financial, not aesthetic reasons.

(Unlike England's CAMRA, the AHA is not a political movement. CAMRA set out to protect two or three distinctive British beer styles and an institution, the "independent local," or pub uncontrolled by the major brewers. They were not interested in home brewing, in part because home brewing by definition takes place outside the pub. From the beginning, the American Homebrewers Association—or Association of Brewers—served both constituencies. As more of its members graduated to micro-brewing, the AHA established a micro-brewing arm, the Institute for Brewing Studies. While the AHA served the home brewers, the IBS held conferences for prospective micro-brewers. Consistently, more than three-quarters of the attendees were home brewers.)

Once settled in Stonesfield, a village of three hundred people, surrounded by barley fields, we tried its three pubs. The nearest was a Courage outlet, the Black Sheep, which was longer on boisterous dart-contest atmosphere than on real ale. Then we headed for the two largest breweries on the list, Morrell's in Oxford and Morland's in Abingdon. Morrell's annual production is 40,000 barrels, and Morland's is 70,000. (The English barrel is thirty-six gallons, whereas an American barrel is thirty-one gallons.) Both head brewers had received our letters and gave us personally conducted tours.

By American standards, Morrell's and Morland's are tiny, about one-twentieth the size of an average U.S. brewery, but compared with my ten-gallon basement brewery, they were enormous. Thanks to my home brewing experience, however, I found it easy and enjoyable to follow the process from grinding through mashing, sparging, boiling, and fermentation to kegging. At the end, the brewers served us some of their products in employees' tap rooms. Both breweries were over a hundred years old, but their equipment was relatively new and thus lacked the architectural romance one associates with an old-fashioned facility.

Tradition greeted us in spades at the Hook Norton Brewery, about thirty miles west of Oxford. Hook Norton is one of the few remaining "tower breweries"—great, classic, five-story wooden structures built in the late nineteenth century. Louvers in the Victorian cupola vented the brew kettles' steam, and on this chill December morning, great clouds wreathed the upper stories.

David Clarke, third-generation brewer and owner, led us through the brewery from top to bottom, just as the grain, hops, and water progress from the tower down to the basement casking operation. "We're dragging ourselves into the nineteenth century," he quipped as he showed us the 1890 steam engine and the 1920s "coppers," or boilers. Only the white plastic fermenting vessels looked contemporary. In the middle of the tour, Clarke paused for five minutes to help an employee add Fuggles and Comet hops and a small amount of dark malt extract to a brew. Then it was down into the basement, where, in a corner, Clarke served us half-pints of his three ales. He drew the beer directly from wooden kegs placed there for the employees. They were all delicious, especially Old Hookey, a well-hopped, darker ale.

We next drove to the rolling Cotswold hills laced with sheep farms and fields of brussels sprouts and barley. In a small valley north of Stow-on-the-Wold, we found a brewery that gave new dimension to the word *idyllic*. In a series of connected stone buildings dating back to the fifteenth century, L. Claude Arkell brews twenty barrels of pale ale daily for his seventeen tied houses and inns. The brewery stands beside a trout pond whose denizens feed on some of the spent grains, while above them float stately black swans, geese, and ducks. Water from the pond turns a mill wheel that is connected to Arkell's grain grinder. Twenty years ago, Arkell harvested his own barley, malted it in one part of the barn, and used the product in his beer. Now he buys the barley locally. Hops come from nearby Worcestershire.

He seemed so devoted to his brewery and so matter-of-fact about its operation that we asked what it would take to start a brewery from scratch and operate it profitably.

"It wouldn't be so hard," Arkell said. "I never went to brewing school. I learned from other brewers, picked their brains, kept my mouth shut. Good brewing is really only four things: get your water chemistry right, watch your brewing temperature, clean the pipes, and use your noddle." He surely made it seem simple and straightforward. What a life—to build a brewery by a trout pond, raise sheep and fruit trees on the hillside, feed the geese and swans at dusk.

Arkell said he spends as much time as he can with other brewers, because he feels he can always learn more. One of them had recently introduced him to some new hops pellets that Arkell now used most of the time.

"You know, the big brewers could crush me in a second," he said. "But they won't, because the influence of CAMRA has made them shy of public censure. I am worried about the growth of home brewing kits, because they aren't taxed. Taxes are what make beer so expensive in the pub.

"I'm a third-generation brewer. If you want to see someone who started from scratch, visit Tom Litt. He buys yeast from me once a week."

Litt was already on our list, so we headed for the village of South Leigh, home of the Mason Arms. We had been intrigued with CAMRA's description of Litt's pub as a "home brewery." There, behind the bar, across from a warm oak log fire, we found him engaged in a lively discussion with a customer. They were talking about the Celebration Ale that Litt had brewed to commemorate the marriage of Prince Charles and Lady Diana.

Litt remembered our letter and invited us to come back in the morning. "In the meantime, these are on the house," he said. He handed each of us a pint of Sowlye (South Leigh) Ale, his one and only brew. It was a fine beer, malty yet hopped enough to be memorable.

When we arrived the next morning, we could see the steam rising from a former stable behind the inn. We found Litt stoking an ancient, rusty, coal-fired boiler. As he scampered between the boiler room, brewhouse, and "cellar" (an enclosed horse stall), he told us how he came to brew.

A farmer's son, Litt had bought the run-down farmhouse in 1964, converted it to an inn, and added a restaurant that was good enough to draw people out of Oxford for luncheon. This success made him restless for more challenge, and in 1974, on a half-serious bet, he assembled some equipment and brewed a seventy-five-gallon batch of beer, which, his surprised friends had to agree, was good. Over the next twelve months, he refined both equipment and recipe until he was satisfied. Only one vessel, the hundred-gallon boiling kettle, was built to order. The rest was surplus equipment: a potato cooker from the army, coolers from a dairy, used kegs from other breweries, and a thirty-year-old coal-fired steam boiler. His total investment was less than $10,000.

Tom Litt exuded enthusiasm and pragmatism. He nursed the boiler as if it were human. He used no special water treatment. His conditioning room, where the beer ages in kegs for six to twelve days, was simply an enclosed and cooled horse stall. When the beer was ready to drink, he rolled the keg across the parking lot and tapped it in a room behind his simple bar.

"There's no mystery in brewing. Just keep the place clean. The trouble with most brewers is that they are never satisfied. They are always trying to change this ingredient or that procedure."

"Do you have any problem with health inspectors?" I asked.

"None at all. They know that if I don't keep the brewery clean the beer will spoil and people won't buy it." As for the tax collector, the district officer had a key to the stable and he could and did come in at odd hours to check the correlation between the ingredients Litt buys and the amount of beer he sells. .

As we watched, Litt climbed a ladder with a five-gallon plastic bucket and emptied its dark syrupy contents into the boiler.

"What's that?" I asked.

"Malt extract."

"Malt extract!" I gasped. "You mean you don't mash?"

"Of course not. Why should I? I can make perfectly good beer with the extracts and save time and trouble and expense."

I reeled at the simplicity of it all. Unless I had a tin tongue, he was making an extract ale fully as good as any mashed version I could produce. What was he doing right, and what was I doing wrong?

As he puttered around the brewery, Litt dictated the recipe for his Sowlye Ale (O.G. 1037):

100 gals. water	3 lbs. liquid yeast from Arkell
100 lbs. Edme liquid	1 pint finings at kegging time
malt extract	Handful of loose Goldings for
3 lbs. Golding hops	finishing hops at the end

Boil for an hour, cool it down using a dairy cooler, pump it into the primary fermenter for 4 days, then into kegs for about 10 days, and it's ready to drink.

Was it the wooden kegs he used that made the beer so good? No, they were lined with stainless steel and gave off no special taste. Was it Litt's careful handling? He was no more careful than I was. Was I exaggerating the ambience of South Leigh, Oxfordshire? Perhaps. But that still did not explain it all. How he made such good beer so simply gnawed at me for the rest of our stay in England.

The key to Litt's financial success lay in his reliance on the brewery for only a portion, in his case roughly one-third, of his income. The inn and restaurant provided the other two-thirds. It would be impossible, he said, to make a living from the brewery alone. Nor would he want to. Litt was quite happy to spend only one day a week brewing enough beer to sell in the following week. His seemed a very civilized existence.

Fifty miles away in London, David Bruce was anything but content with a hundred gallons a week. Bruce is the founder of five brewpubs, four in London and one in Bristol. His menagerie of pubs are named The Fox and Firkin, Goose and Firkin, Frog and Firkin, etc. A former manager at Courage's and Theakston's (a small Yorkshire brewery), Bruce took a third mortgage on his London house to launch the first Firkin and in four years was grossing $4 million annually.

By the time Bruce got to London in 1978, there were only four brewpubs extant in England, one of them in the city. Bruce believed that the public was ready for a new round of brewpubs if done with flair. He bought old, mostly run-down pubs and put breweries in the cellars. One pub featured a porthole, another a glass section in the floor through which customers could watch the beer being brewed. Bruce sold beers with such arresting names as Dogbolter, Earthstopper, and Sphincter Special. He produced T-shirts and buttons and formed clubs of regular drinkers. In short, "We're a marketing organization as much as a production organization," said the chief lieutenant, Andy MacDonald.

When we told him that the visit to South Leigh had aroused our interest in tiny commercial brewing, Bruce told us to drive down to Ringwood and see the brewery there. "They've made beer for us when we've run short. What's more, they are selling whole brewery kits—plans, equipment, and all. They even take on students."

The Ringwood Brewery was located in a couple of unpretentious stucco buildings on a back street. The mash tun and boiler with their wooden insulating jackets looked more like hot tubs than brewing vessels. The kegging operation brought to mind the disarray of a bus company repair shop. Ringwood brews its own beer and distributes it to the free trade (nontied houses) nearby, but its bread and butter has been selling the plans and, when possible, the actual equipment for micro-breweries across Great Britain. The cost was roughly $40,000 for plans and equipment for a brewery with a capacity of ten to fifteen barrels. When we visited Ringwood, they had sold about a dozen brewery kits.

Two other factors made the trip to Ringwood worthwhile. It was the first time we had heard of beer sold right out of the brewery. Customers brought their own jugs or purchased them from the brewery and took them home full of porter, bitter, Forty-Niner, or Old Thumper. This retail share of the business had risen to 25 percent in just one year. Ringwood's ales were respectable, but not as good as Hook Norton's or Arkell's.

The second discovery at Ringwood was the name of an American who had served an apprenticeship there. He was William Newman, of Albany, New York, who had fallen in love with English ale and decided to build a brewery in the United States. In 1979, he had worked at Ringwood for four months and then bought the plans for his own operation. The vision of an American single-handedly proposing to blow foam literally and figuratively in the face of the American giants was most intriguing. We would go see him when we returned home.

"Many Are Called . . ."

In the first months after we returned from Britain, I read a number of articles about small breweries in the United States. Almost every issue of *Zymurgy* and *Brewers Digest* included reports of "micro-breweries" in California or Colorado or Oregon. These new breweries produced from several hundred to over a thousand barrels per year, except for Anchor Brewing Company, in San Francisco, which sold about 25,000 barrels of the incomparable Anchor Steam Beer and Anchor Porter. All the micro-breweries in the country hardly threatened the giants. With annual production of 59 million barrels, Budweiser made more beer in three hours than did all the micro-breweries in a year.

In contrast to the hundreds and thousands of employees at the big breweries, the micros were often one- and two-person operations, founded by former home brewers who were longer on love and ingenuity than money. Nonetheless, the articles painted pictures of near-universal success. "We're selling all we can make," was a recurrent comment one read in numerous articles.

There's a bit of the host in each of us. I had once dreamed of running a restaurant. This fantasy stemmed from my grandfather's experience in Helena, Montana, a hundred years ago. He and his brother, immigrants from Bohemia, had established a recreational area called Central Park outside Helena, the state capital. By trolley or horse, citizens had ridden out of town to enjoy baseball fields, a bandstand, a small zoo, and a beer garden serving schooners and kegs of lager from the nearby Horsky and Kessler breweries. Now that I was a brewer, my imagination leaped to the same kind of hospitality, only this included pouring tankards of my own ale, lager, and stout.

During the next months, I offered more and more of my beer to friends and strangers. This was low-cost market research, which, in a way, I had performed since my first offerings of Prohibition Pilsner. Those who liked it, I asked: Would you ever pay money for this beer? How much? What kind of container would you like to see? How important is the label or what the advertising says? Those (blissfully) few who admitted to not liking the beer, I asked how it might be improved.

And the public. Wouldn't it respond enthusiastically to a beer made in Vermont, with its image of purity, hard work, and virtue? Wouldn't the tourists and out-of-state students who flocked the hills and slopes for hiking and skiing, also crowd the bars to drink fine hand-crafted Vermont brews? If I made an intriguing enough label, wouldn't they then take the bottles home to Boston or New York as collectors' items?

About this time, my brother sent me an article from the packaging-industry trade journal *Beverage World*. Under the title "The Bell Doesn't Toll for All Small Breweries," Harold O. Davidson voiced unexpected optimism about the future of small breweries. In contrast to the general expectation of further concentration within the industry, Davidson pointed to a limit on economies of scale. Beyond a certain figure, it would become too expensive to transport a product of 96 percent water. This limitation provided an opening for small and regional breweries. Citing a study by the Stanford Research Institute, Davidson foresaw a "micro-segmentation" within the industry. The market, he forecast, would split into specialized sectors and progressively subdivide as an increased percentage of the population followed more individualistic buying patterns. In other words, more people were becoming open to more flavorful beers, and they were ready to vote their palates and not be led by mass advertising gimmicks. I was encouraged to believe that such micro-breweries might have a chance, depending upon how and where they marketed their products.

Enough dreaming. Albany was only four hours away, and home to the fledgling William S. Newman Brewing Company. It was time to visit one of these breweries.

In a weedy, seedy industrial area a mile from downtown Albany, Chris and I found Newman's brewery. Only a bright new green-and-white sign announcing BREWERY distinguished the building from half a dozen other run-down brick warehouses nearby. The structure had been a mattress factory until fire gutted its innards, leaving it abandoned for thirty years. William Newman was a tall, lean, intense man in tie, sweater, heavy trousers, and rubber boots. A former newspaper editor, teacher, laborer, and state budget analyst, Newman explained that his inspiration arose from an English vacation when he called on small breweries.

After visits to several small American breweries, like D. G. Yuengling & Sons in Pottsville, Pennsylvania, and Anchor Brewing Company in San Francisco, Newman went back to England for his four-month Ringwood apprenticeship. Upon his return to Albany, he spent half a year assembling his construction and financing package. His biggest problem was not raising the money ($250,000 of bank financing, city and state development loans, and his own savings) or formulating a brew, but finding a suitable location. His first choice, in a light industrial zone, adjoined a Fundamentalist church. Unhappy at the prospect of a brewery next door, the congregation successfully opposed his permit application. Newman turned to the abandoned mattress factory.

As I entered the building, I was greeted by a jerry-rigged bar in one corner and the entrance to a small office in another. Copying Ringwood's practice, Newman sold beer straight from the keg in returnable plastic containers. He said this method already accounted for a third of his sales. From there we passed into his newly painted and insulated "brewhouse," which contained the boiling vessel, hops separator, and four thousand-gallon fermenters. The largest room in the 10,000-square-foot building served a mixture of purposes: grain storage and grinding, a six-hundred-gallon mash tun, and keg washing and filling. Newman had decided to keg his entire production. "It's cheaper and simpler," he said. "I'm surprised that other small breweries are bottling. When you bottle, you have to buy all the containers. You need bottle soakers, fillers, crowners, labelers. And the time involved! Small-scale bottling equipment is hard to find. And then how do you maintain it?"

Total production time, from grinding grain to tapping a keg at a bar, was two and a half weeks. Newman's Pale Ale used Ringwood's recipe and yeast. The barley was American, while the hops were a mixture of American, British, and German varieties.

Newman said that the Albany area had a higher-than-average draft beer consumption rate, and he hoped this would help make his beer the local favorite. Since his beer tasted best around 50° F., he insisted that the bars serve it at that temperature, or else buy a specially built cooler that could do the job. Furthermore, he required that they wait at least twelve hours before serving the beer, so that the yeast could settle. (It seemed to me that these strictures might reduce sales, but I didn't say anything.)

From the brewery we went next door to the Thatcher Street Pub, a working class bar and one of Newman's best customers. We ordered hamburgers while Newman fetched a fistful of steins and sat down opposite us. As we raised glasses, my mind suddenly went back to the first time I had offered my beer to friends. Bill Newman had the same look on his face. Suppose the beer was terrible. What should I say? I began dredging my vocabulary for words of comfort and praise.

I took a sip. Whew! I brightened. It tasted like . . . Ringwood's Forty-Niner. "Tasty," I said diplomatically. Newman relaxed. It was quite akin to the other traditional ales we had drunk in England. I liked it, but I wondered how it would sell in American Lagerland. How long would it take for Albany palates to adjust to the taste, slight cloudiness, and warmer temperature of Newman's Pale Ale? Newman obviously hoped it would be before his money ran out. There was a precedent—yogurt had caught on in the land of cottage cheese.

My next step was to call the executive secretary of the Brewers Association of America, the trade association for smaller breweries. William O'Shea, a lawyer and brewery advocate by profession, had run the association for over forty years. Nicknamed "Mr. Small Brewery," he also had the sobriquet of "the industry's undertaker" because he had watched the demise of hundreds of American breweries over those four decades. Surely, I thought, he would be sympathetic to questions about starting a small brewery.

If he was, he expressed it in an odd way. After I outlined my dream, he said bluntly, "You're crazy. People come in here or call every week with the idea they are going to build a small brewery, and they don't have a clue about how tough the market is, or what's required to be success-ful." He dismissed most of the micro-brewers, or "boutique brewers," as hobbyists who would do little to help the industry. He did concede that one of these new brewers, Jack McAuliffe of the New Albion Brewery in California, had "the right attitude and the necessary mechanical skills to succeed. He built all his own equipment."

"What about Fritz Maytag of Anchor Brewing?" I asked.

"Oh, he's a special case. He knew what he was doing from the beginning."

No one likes to be called a fool, and I smarted from his criticism; if he was an industry spokesman, the industry was hurting. But later, after talking to several small brewers, I realized this judgment was unfair. O'Shea, these men said, had been a determined and resourceful defend-er of local and regional brewers. His bluntness bespoke a deep under-standing of the difficulties involved and the battle scars from his decades-long rearguard action.

O'Shea gave me one thing besides a chill shower: he confirmed that Maytag and McAuliffe were two of the founding fathers of this micro-brewing movement. Anchor Steam was a world-class beer, as distinctive as Guinness or Pilsner Urquell. Of New Albion I knew zero. There was nothing for it but to visit these pioneers.

The Anchor Brewing Company is housed in a cream-colored former cof-fee factory in a mixed light industrial and residential neighborhood of San Francisco. You climb a flight of stairs to the office and find yourself looking directly onto the brewing floor. Across from the two office desks through a glass partition gleam the cones and chimneys of three copper vessels. Through another glass wall is the taproom, whose walls are fes-tooned with old brewing advertising signs, photographs of steam beer breweries, and glass cases of brewing instruments and utensils. A carved oak bar serves beer to visitors and coffee or tea to employees.

One whole corner is devoted to souvenirs, such as belt buckles, T-shirts, aprons, and visors, all bearing the attractive red, blue, green, tan, and white emblem of "Anchor Steam Beer—Made in San Francisco since 1896."

I was shown into a room where a man was on his hands and knees, as intent as a child shooting marbles. He was flipping a two-inch-thick stack of three-by-four-foot sheets of bottle labels. In his well-tailored clothes, he looked more like a Boston investment banker than a brewer. But behind the rimless hexagonal glasses, his eyes were restless, quizzical, and determined. Speaking almost to himself, he said he must decide in twenty-four hours whether the printer should proceed with these 8 million labels, which was a year's supply. "Do you realize how many eight million bottles are?" he asked. He was thinking out loud. The blue in the label still did not quite match the blue in the bottle cap: "The color is drifting too much." He wanted them just right. He gave word to have the printer try one more match.

"Now, what can I do for you?" Fritz Maytag asked.

I said I was one more home brewing moth drawn to the light of commercial brewing and I had come to learn how he'd made Anchor such a successful company.

We sat down at a table where I could look out onto the copper brewing kettles and he told me his story.

In 1965, Fritz Maytag, heir to the washing machine fortune, with a degree in Asian studies from Stanford, was, as he put it, "drifting." He had helped start a dairy business and winery in Chile, and he didn't want to go back to the family trade in Iowa. During a visit to San Francisco, he went to dinner at one of his college haunts, the Spaghetti Factory, where as a student he had drunk schooners of Anchor Steam Beer, a local brew and the last of a great tradition of steam beers.

Steam beer is to beer what the banjo is to musical instruments—America's only genuine contribution to the field. The name is derived from the strong carbonation in the beer when it ferments. It is a hybrid beverage first brewed during the Gold Rush days in the mid-nineteenth century, using lager yeast but at warmer ale-fermenting temperatures. The brewers also included the German-Bohemian system of kraeusening—adding some young beer to the aging beer to give it natural carbonation. When kegs of steam beer were tapped, they hissed and foamed in a manner unlike English-style ales. Spectators to the tapping applied the misnomer *steam* to the beer. California then had little or no ice or deep cellars in which to keep the beer cool. At one time, there had been twenty-seven steam beer breweries in San Francisco. By Prohibition, this number had fallen to seven, and by 1965 there was only Anchor, producing fewer than five hundred barrels a year.

At the Spaghetti Factory, Maytag heard that Anchor was for sale. The next day, he visited the brewery and, on an impulse, bought it lock, stock, and lauter tun.

"It was a crazy thing to do. The brewery was a disaster. The equipment was ghastly. The quality was inconsistent. When it was good, it was very good. At its worst, it was pretty bad. Some of the bad beer was getting into the trade and making a poor sales situation worse. They made a batch about every two months. They didn't even boil the wort; they just sort of simmered it. They sold only draft, and the kegs were dirty and leaked."

At first, Maytag simply paid the bills and tried to halt the sales decline. But then he decided he either had to get out or get into the business all the way and make a going concern of it. "I was determined to see this brewery succeed as a real business. I wanted to sell beer at a reasonable price. I wanted to make a real beer, not a gimmick or a joke or a hype.

"I can't say that I bought the brewery with a lot of philosophical intent. It's true that from the first I was infatuated with the mystery of brewing, its alchemical aspects. There is something magical in our culture about the idea of alcohol and mind-altering substances that is moderately accepted. It is a dreadful thing in many ways. A lot of people have been killed by alcohol. Scary stuff. But I think it does a lot more good than harm. Beer is the common man's alcohol. Breweries are places where you literally create beer out of grain—it's really alchemy—turning grain into bubbly, sparkling, magic stuff that affects your attitude— makes you sing songs . . . and cry.

"Setting out to make a high-quality product was my theme from the beginning. I wanted a sense of security about the product because of the way it was made, the methods, equipment, etc. I wanted an old-fashioned, interesting, unusual way of brewing, a story I could talk about. I took what little we had at the brewery and what I could learn about this funny West Coast tradition of steam beer and cast a Platonic ideal of what Anchor Steam Beer would be like if you had all the technology to make it simple and pure."

But to make it pure wasn't so simple. "It took years of building and testing, lots of money on rent and salaries to develop the beer and then sell it as a great local product."

Maytag took a number of brewing courses, but for the most part he taught himself on the job and through reading. He worked on the equipment. He made sure of what was needed and then spent the money to get it—stainless steel and copper everywhere. He received help from people in the dairy industry who had long experience with sanitation.

"We're doing something very weird, which is making beer at warm temperatures—fifties and sixties—and holding it for a month. Sanitation must be our main concern. No brewery can be dirty and make good beer. There are very few organisms which grow in beer, but, boy, do they grow! The way we are doing it, we're asking for trouble—it's like leaving the apple pie to cool on the back porch for a week."

The vessels in which primary fermentation occurs are unique to brewing, being twenty-by-thirty-foot stainless-steel open pans, two and a half feet deep at one end and three and a half feet deep at the other.

It took Maytag five years to build up his sales from 500 to 1,200 barrels annually. In another three years, he reached 7,000 and the company moved into the black for the first time. He began distributing in the Western states, Minnesota, and New Jersey. Anchor was becoming a cult beer. He added an Anchor Porter and pushed the old brewery to its limit of 12,000 barrels.

In 1977, Maytag bought a used German brewhouse with a capacity of 40,000 barrels. He had it shipped to a new, larger building in San Francisco. In a couple of years, he was producing 18,000 barrels to break even, and by 1982 Anchor was distributing 28,500 barrels of steam and porter to twenty states. This is still less than one-thousandth of Budweiser's annual production, but, then, Maytag is assuredly not competing with Budweiser. Anchor is a strong, all-malt brew with four times the hops of the average American beer.

When I told him of my brewery fantasy, Maytag laughed and said scores of people had come to see him with the same dream.

"I try to talk to them all. I tell them that first it takes a lot of money. Industry estimates are a hundred to two hundred dollars per barrel of capacity installed. I think you have to look on the high side of that figure. I could never have done this without inherited money, because no one would lend me the funds. I don't care how charming I was or how good the beer tasted. This is a risky business. The whole country, the whole world, is full of empty breweries.

"Secondly, you need at least one person who will devote unbelievable effort to making good beer. Even so, it takes a lot of luck and a lot of talent, because you can't make a good reputation quickly for a product unless you're very lucky.

"When I took over this brewery, there were only a few imports here, mainly Dos Equis, Guinness, and Heineken. The wine and cheese renaissances hadn't yet taken place, the greening of America was still to come, the whole 'good life' movement hadn't occurred. Americans didn't know yet that they were going to start to enjoy food and drink and savor quality and natural things.

"Beer is just beer. That's part of the problem and part of the fun of it. Wine is anything you want to make of it, but beer is beer. That's one reason I like making beer. On the one hand, it's the common man's drink. Nobody will pay a dollar a bottle for any great quantity of it. On the other hand, it's much harder to make than wine, takes more art and science. The biggest difference from wine is that beer lacks what I call the participation and risks of nature. Classic wine is made from grapes in one location. In good years they're great and in bad years they're bad. When you drink that wine, you participate in that risk.

"To build a successful brewery, you needn't spend as much money as I did, but you do have to sell your product, and that's something home brewers don't realize. We put in a lot of hours, years, selling here and then moving to Wyoming, Arizona, Boston, and Florida. In the whole Bay Area we sell maybe two thousand barrels. The reason we range so far is that we can't sell enough here. The beer doesn't sell itself."

Maytag did not spend a lot of money on advertising, certainly nothing to compete with the majors. Instead, he assiduously cultivated opinion makers, newspaper writers, and the public through guided brewery tours. He made sure Anchor was entered in beer tastings around California. Anchor's reputation spread, as beer lovers learned about the funny little dark "steam" beer that held its own against the more heavily advertised European imports.

Probably the most important lesson Maytag learned from all his reading and experimentation was to have near-operating-room cleanliness in his brewhouse. The average visitor looks at the shining brew kettles through the window of the hospitality room, then turns to drink some beer. The alert home brewer will notice the fanatical maintenance.

Maytag went first-class on his equipment, not because he wanted to impress people but because of the need for sanitation. "Home brewers don't have this kind of problem. They brew maybe once a week, then put their equipment away until the next batch. If you take a shower once a week, you can have a pretty decrepit shower stall, even a wooden one with a canvas floor. After using it on Saturday night, it will be dry by Monday. Mold won't grow and rot it. But take three showers a day every day, and that shower will literally walk away after a year. In a commercial brewery everything is wet, and unless you clean well every day, you pick up mold and bacteria and wild yeast."

Maytag's polite demeanor turns scornful when he talks about people who think of brewing more as an art than as a science.

"Let me tell you my dirty-thumbprint theory. A group of people go to a little, seedy, dirty Mexican restaurant with fantastic tacos and tortillas. Back in the kitchen, there's the mama making tortillas. But they notice that her hands are dirty. They then conclude that the tortillas are good because they're made by a real woman who is kind of sloppy. Well, I don't buy it. The tortillas are good because the flour is the best or because the warmth of her hand provides the best temperature. It is not because of the dirt."

About sixty miles from Maytag's splendid brewery, down a dusty Sonoma road lined with vineyards, I found the New Albion Brewing Company, occupying half of a twenty-by-forty gray metal warehouse. Only a small hand-lettered sign wired to a piece of rusting farm machinery hinted this was a pioneer brewery.

The office was a stark contrast to that of Anchor Brewing. In one corner of the ten-foot-square space was an enormous open safe, inside of which were a pile of brewing texts. Another corner contained advertising and promotional materials, T-shirts, placards, and tabletop displays. The rest of the room was taken up by a large desk covered by books, papers, and two sleeping cats.

Jack McAuliffe had discovered British ales while stationed at an American submarine base in northern Scotland in the 1960s. When he had run short of money to spend at pubs, he found a home brew supply shop nearby and began making his own beer. By the time he left the navy, McAuliffe had decided to build his own small brewery.

Through eight or nine jobs, including one as an optical engineer in Silicon Valley, McAuliffe nurtured his dream. He chose the name New Albion for his beers because that was the name Sir Francis Drake gave to the San Francisco Bay area when he stopped there on his global circumnavigation in 1579. Drake's ship, the *Golden Hind*, continued its voyage on the New Albion labels.

McAuliffe was as different from Maytag as a bulldog from a greyhound. Whereas Maytag was almost professorial in dress and demeanor, McAuliffe was blue-collar through and through. Whereas Maytag chose his words carefully, McAuliffe spat them out brusquely. Whereas Maytag assembled an immaculate four-story brewery in San Francisco, McAuliffe's reflected his shade-tree mechanical skills. He had built the brewery from government surplus fifty-five-gallon stainless-steel drums. Every piece of equipment, except for a surplus bottle washer (which he bought for $150), he fabricated himself, including a malt hopper, all the fermentation tanks, and the boiler. The grinding mill he built from scratch, using a design from an 1852 brewing text. He trucked in his brewing water every two weeks from a "secret" spring in the hills above Sonoma. With that water he brewed between five and ten barrels a week, or about 350 barrels per year.

"How did you begin?" I asked.

"You're a home brewer," he said. "You know how it is when you and your buddies suck down a couple of your beers and say, 'Jesus, wouldn't it be wonderful to do this for a living?' I like beer. I like making beer. Where else could I pick the labels, the bottles, and the name, choose the recipes, decide who will work for me and who will interview me? Where else could I have kittens on the desk? A brewery is the natural consequence of making your own beer. Now, I've always liked the flow of water, ever since I played in creeks as a kid. And I'm mechanical by nature. Unless you're wealthy beyond the dreams of avarice, you must have mechanical ability. And even if you have all the money you need, you still need that understanding of the process. I like to say that farmers make wine and engineers make beer. You must know water and pumps and numbers. And sanitation is *numero uno*.

"Many people think there's an unlimited demand for this product. Wrong. We make a specialty beer, strongly flavored, more beery than most. To sell that kind of beer in a bar, you have to have one which is not just good, it must be great and elbow the other guys aside. It's a mighty competitive business, and successful brewers play hardball. To run a micro-brewery, you need the technical skills to get it out the door. Then you need all the financial knowledge and business skills of running any small business, because brewing is first and foremost a business."

As an example of micro-brewery frustrations, McAuliffe explained that he'd originally gone through the traditional distribution system. "However, our beer didn't have the shelf life or the volume of the larger brands. Distributors are the same as in any business—they have no interest in any product *per se*. The only thing they are interested in is how much money they are making. So, if you have a product that's delicate, different, high class, and low volume, you get pushed over into the corner under the fluorescent bulb. And then, when someone on the route wants it, they look around and bring out some which has been sitting there under the worst possible conditions. So we just cut the Gordian knot and went directly to our local retail customers. Want a beer?"

Without waiting for an answer, he fetched two glasses and drew them full from a tap fitted into the wall between his bottling and fermentation rooms. It was mellow, a bit cloudy, and stronger than Newman's Pale Ale. It combined the colder temperature and carbonation expected in America with the full body and aroma of genuine English ale.

After I complimented him on the beer, I asked about the future of micro-breweries in this country.

"First there is the image, the romance, the dream. Then there is the reality. As the industry continues to shrink, the products have tended to taste more and more like one another. In this country there is a choice of brands but no choice of style. The larger breweries are brewing for the mass market; they can't afford to make specialty beers.

"However, people are becoming more interested in food that tastes different, and that broadened taste will support more specialty beers. The micro-breweries can fill that niche. But they need help in getting their beers onto market shelves."

I told him of all the home brewers I knew who were fascinated with building and running their own breweries, myself included. McAuliffe gave me a long ironic look and said, "Many are called, that's for sure. How many are *chosen* is yet to be seen."

I left New Albion with a couple of T-shirts, a bottle of beer, and a knapsack of admiration for him. Jack McAuliffe was the sandlot brewer who had turned pro. We home brewers could admire Maytag's systematic, conscientious resurrection of the moribund Anchor brewery, and we envied the financial resources which allowed him to buy the best equipment. But it was easier to identify with the perseverance, ingenuity, and outright brass of Jack McAuliffe, the solitary, dedicated junk rat and entrepreneur who designed and built his brewery from scratch.

Still, the mote in my mind's eye was whether he could survive. Despite tens of thousands of dollars of free publicity, early entry into the market, and, from all I had heard and could judge, an excellent if sometimes inconsistent product, McAuliffe had never produced more than 350 barrels of beer a year. It was something to ponder.

I had one more stop in California—Bill Owens, the founder of Buffalo Bill's Brewpub. Owens, a former photographer and home brewer, had built the second brewpub in the U.S. and he was an indefatigable champion of this type of brewery. He had even trademarked the name "brewpub." Owens argued that beer was going through the same kind of taste revolution which had occurred in coffee, mustard, pasta, and bread. People were searching for more sophisticated flavors *AND* they wanted to drink that beer in places where they didn't have to compete with drunks, sports nuts, or truck drivers. What Owens offered was fresh, unfiltered, unpasteurized beer which had only traveled sixty-two feet from the conditioning tank to the bar tap. Customers could watch Owens or his assistant brewer making batches through a glass wall. (He stirred his mash tun with a canoe paddle.) Owens stressed the ambience of the place: no smoking, but some darts, music, and good solid food.

To raise the money for the initial brewpub, Owens sold shares for $2,500 apiece. Despite his marketing skill and a raft of media attention, the shares "did not sell like hotcakes. It took 1000 phone calls and over a year to sell twenty-seven units" and launch the operation.

Owens was in the middle of raising money for his second brewpub, this one closer to the Bay Area. He had dreams of developing a string of these brewpubs along the entire California coast, much "like the early Spanish missions," he joked. (For a couple of days, I even toyed with the

idea of buying a share in the second Buffalo Bill Brewpub. It would certainly be cheaper than doing my own. However, when I called Bill to
inquire, he told me that, alas, investors had to be California residents.)
Meanwhile, several other brewpubs were under development.

The capital investment for a brewpub was certainly less than for a
regular brewery. The profit on a barrel of beer was, Owens contended,
four, five, or even six times that of bottled beer.

Of course, by definition, a brewpub included a restaurant, with all its
attendant specialized demands and quirks. And the question I needed to
have answered was: which was more important—the restaurant or the
brewery? In a brewery, you could be an introvert and just brew beer, but
in a brewpub you had to be an extrovert and make sure the customers
were happy.

Owens had never been to England, never visited Tom Litt or David
Bruce, the English brewpublicans. He had created his own distinctive
American style of brewpub.

Next stop: New York City.

"Why would a successful thirty-one-year-old executive with a major
corporation risk his life savings on a project that almost guarantees he
will never be rich?" asked the press release. Because, the ad said rhetor-
ically, Matthew P. Reich had a mission to "bring a distinctive, flavorful,
American beer to the American market."

I met Reich in a pinched little office on the lower West Side where
he was overseeing the delivery of his beer to delis in Manhattan. At first,
Reich had believed his own public relations and assumed it would be
easy to raise the $1 million he needed to build his brewery. When he
found he could raise no more than a quarter of that, one of his potential
investors suggested that he subcontract the beermaking at an existing
brewery. Reich was intrigued. "I had seen the kinds of bacterial infection
other micro-brewers were having. By having a large brewery produce my
beer, I would be free to concentrate on marketing. Once you have a good
product, the key is marketing. Word of mouth is not enough by itself. A
reputation has to be cultured, the way Maytag did it. You have to send
your beer to the right people, get the right personalities to write about it."

Reich convinced brewing consultant Joseph Owades to help him for-
mulate New Amsterdam Amber Beer, an all-malt lager with 80 percent
pale and 20 percent crystal malt and fresh Cascade and Hallertau hops.

It would ferment at the relatively high temperature of 65° F. The two went to F. X. Matt, president of the West End Brewing Co. in Utica, New York. Matt liked the idea, and, having excess brewing capacity, he agreed to begin producing five-hundred-barrel batches of New Amsterdam.

Reich's market research told him to aim for two male cohorts, the eighteen-to-twenty-four-year-old college crowd and the twenty-four-to-forty-year-old young professionals who drank imported beer for status and flavor. He sold his "connoisseur's beer" in single bottles, in delicatessens and saloons where the customers would be "insensitive" to price. Reich said he expected to be selling eight thousand barrels in three years, by which time he would have raised the money to build his own brewery.

The notion of contracting the beer made great sense—commission an established brewery to make the beer to your specifications. That brewery would know sanitation thoroughly. Then, if the beer didn't sell, the investors, including Reich, would lose only the year's cash flow, not the much larger sum needed for plant and equipment.

After my tour of Newman, Anchor, New Albion, Buffalo Bill's, and New Amsterdam, I remained enthusiastic but was more respectful of the difficulties in becoming a small-time brewer. All recognized the importance of marketing and the complexities of a small business. I admired them for different reasons: Maytag because his beer was the best; McAuliffe because he had built his brewery out of little but sweat and mechanical skill; Newman because he had so much faith in the English-style ales to which I was partial; Owens because of his irrepressible advocacy of brewpubs; and Reich because he opened my eyes to the possibilities of contract brewing.

All five American brewers had added the yeast of their experience to the wort of my fantasies. After this concoction fermented, it would be time to subject it to more severe analysis.

Savage Commitment

The union of the mathematician with the poet,
Fervor with measure, passion with correctness,
That surely is the ideal.

—William James

For several months, I nursed the dream of my own brewery. The last Vermont brewery, Petersen's in Burlington, had closed its taps in 1894. Ninety-plus years was long enough for a beer drought. What's more, with Vermont's established reputation for good cheese, maple syrup, ice cream, and craftsmanship of all kinds, the state begged to have a small brewery offering real ale or lager. Not only would the residents love the beer, but the sixty million people living within a day's drive would surely thirst for a Green Mountain brew. Once I had the tourists hooked, they would do my marketing, carrying the message (and the demand) home to Massachusetts, Connecticut, New York, and beyond.

Everyone I spoke with thought the idea was terrific. But talk was cheap and I knew I couldn't do this alone. I needed to find other people as committed as I, people with serious purpose and . . . deep pockets. Therefore, I invited a selection of friends over one evening to explore the idea of building a small brewery. They were all people who liked my beer or who were home brewers themselves. They included a lawyer, an investment advisor, an engineering student, a contractor, a community organizer, Barton Merle-Smith, the hot tubs entrepreneur, and the former manager of a whey-processing plant and now a food-equipment broker.

For an hour the conversation ranged across possible names for the brewery, the types of beer we could make, possible locations, vague cost estimates, and customer profiles. I extolled Anchor, New Albion, and

Reich's rental-brewery scheme. I told them of the micro-segmentation of the market and the growth of imported beer sales, as well as the home brewing revolution. The more home brew we drank, the more the idea glittered. But during a pause in the jollity, Jim Hinkel raised his hand. He said he had scribbled some notes just before the meeting and he wanted to share them.

"First, I think you need to define the reasons for this venture. Is it to be a hobby or a business? Will it stand alone, or be part of something else, such as a restaurant or pub?

"Second, you must lay out the financial factors in *pro forma*s for at least three years. When do you expect to make a profit? How do you plan to raise the money? Have you *talked* to any banks?

"Third, there are marketing questions. Where will your beer fit into the present market? What share do you expect to get in Vermont, in New England, in three years, in five years, in ten years? Who are your competitors? Are you challenging Budweiser, or Genesee, or Heineken? What is your sales plan? You need at least a three-year unit-pricing forecast. What promotional programs do you have in mind?"

I gulped and looked around the room. The others were squirming, too, but Hinkel wasn't finished.

"Fourth, there are construction factors. What are the state and federal regulations on building a brewery? Will you need a special permit for dumping waste water? Have you considered the taxes on a brewery? What size brewery will you build? Can you find equipment off the shelf, or must it all be custom-made? What is your construction budget? Remember, whatever you calculate, expect it to double.

"Fifth, what are your personnel requirements? If you spend all your time brewing, who will manage the operation? How will you train your help? What will you pay them?"

Hinkel paused to catch his breath. "Those are just a few notes. I haven't even touched on financing, distributors, suppliers, utilities, et cetera, et cetera."

The et ceteras tolled like a clock on Death Row. Jim Hinkel wasn't telling me to go back to the drawing board; in his opinion, I hadn't even entered the drafting room.

After recovering from Hinkel's cold shower of realism, I realized that I should probably not discuss a brewery over beer. It was also obvious that far more serious study was called for. I began plowing through some brewing textbooks, with the sinking feeling I would have to learn a lot of microbiology. I talked to as many micro-brewers as I could find. When the American Homebrewers Association expanded its annual convention to include micro-brewing workshops, I joined scores of people in Boulder for lectures on malt, equipping a brewery, mashing theory, packaging, beer styles, and hops utilization. The group ranged across the spectrum from glassy-eyed hippies from out of the mountains to a Virginia veterinarian who brewed so frequently that he had refrigerated an entire room for storage and was now trying to raise $300,000 for the giant step into commercial brewing. David Bruce flew in from London to talk about his brewpubs. I went home with my spirits rekindled. I started looking for short courses in brewing science, microbiology, and something about financial projections and packaging.

But then I took a detour from my brewing career—onto the road of politics. I won election to the Vermont House of Representatives. Even though the office was a part-time duty, there was no way I could do much about a brewery during those two years. Re-election further postponed my commercial brewing career.

While I wrestled with the issues of income taxes, welfare reform, banking regulation, school financing, and minimum sentencing, others were building breweries all across the country. Several of the people I had met in Boulder were among them. In California, breweries sprang up like Topsy. Portland, Oregon, was another hotbed of micro-brewing. In Helena, Montana, several entrepreneurs bought the Kessler name and launched a new Kessler beer. It was hard to keep track of these new breweries dotting the landscape. Here in Vermont, Steve Mason, a former physical education instructor, and home brewer Alan Davis launched Catamount Brewing Company. Steve had brought some sample brews and his plans to our home brew club. The beer was well balanced, hoppy, and flavorful. But Jim Hinkel had just singed our ears with skepticism, so we passed those sentiments on to Steve. He and Alan were undaunted, and their brewery opened its spigots. When I bought my first six-pack at the local market, my envy was washed away in the delight of drinking well-crafted specialty beers made in our own backyard. A brewing revolution was under way.

Such enthusiasm over brewery births was tempered by the obituaries. Charles Coury of the Cartwright Brewing Company in Portland believed that his seventeen years of winemaking would make brewing "as easy as falling off a log. I was a little arrogant. The differences in degree were so great they became differences in kind. I wish I could have labeled the beer Brew Number One, Number Two, et cetera, and then on the back of the label asked for comments. Everyone expected the first beer to be perfect. In retrospect, it takes quite a bit of wasted beer to break in the equipment and get the right taste." After a year and a half and $100,000, he closed.

Fred Eckhardt, who had acted as an informal adviser to Coury, commented, "The things he wanted to do, he didn't have the equipment for. The things he should have done, he didn't recognize the need for. So he went more than a year trying to solve technical problems and competing with people he shouldn't have competed with. His market was people with a taste that says, 'Love me or hate me.' He finally got around to changing the formula, and it was pretty good. But by then it was too late."

Matthew Reich went ahead and built a brewery in New York City, where he brewed for two years, but finally sold the label to his former contractor, F. X. Matt. Reich, who has since moved on to organizing international bicycle races, said he was defeated by the costs of brewing in Manhattan. He could make an operating profit, but ". . . a return on investment? No. It's just that the overhead in New York is different from that in Norwalk, Connecticut. It's a different animal."*

William Newman found, to his woe, that his style of beer and distribution system were out of step with American drinking habits. Also failing to find the money for a bottling line, Newman was forced to lease his brewing equipment to another brewery and to begin contracting for his own beers.

There were other failures. River City Brewing Company in Sacramento and the first Boulder Brewing Company both were overwhelmed by the relentless forces of the market.

"We found that making beer, despite its many difficulties, was the easy part, maybe fifteen percent of the business," said one of Boulder's

---

* *American Brewer,* Spring 1992, p. 15.

founders. "Forget the romance of experimenting with different kinds of hops and malts. You've got more important things to think about, like keeping the beer free of bacteria and then selling what you make."

Saddest of all was the demise of New Albion. Jack McAuliffe was never able to get his production and consistency up to profit-making levels, and he couldn't raise the capital to expand. This was dismaying news, for I sensed that no one had worked harder than McAuliffe. New Albion's passing was like the death of a prophet.

In the middle of these mixed reports, I helped to found a brewpub, and it didn't cost me a dime. One day, while at work in the legislature, I got a call from Greg Noonan in Massachusetts. I recognized the name from the fine technical manual he had written on making lager beer. He wanted to build a brewpub in Vermont, probably in Burlington, but he needed the law changed to permit it. Could I help?

"Sure," said I, happy to work on something besides banking regulation and a gathering battle between the state and the electric power industry.

Existing laws, passed after Prohibition, proscribed "tied-houses" or brewery-owned bars, the general practice in England. These laws required a three-tiered system of brewery, distributor, and retailer. Vermont law said that no second-class licensee—that is, someone who sells beer for off-premise consumption—could also make the beer. Knowing that there are usually several ways to skin a legislative cat, we turned the problem upside down. What if a brewery (manufacturer) could have a retail license to sell beer on its premises? After a certain amount of drafting acrobatics, that idea found favor with the Liquor Control Board, and then progressively with four legislative committees, both legislative chambers, and finally the governor. In late 1988, the Vermont Pub and Brewery opened its doors (and taps). Burlington had its first brewery in ninety-four years.

ARE YOU SERIOUS?

In the following pages, I will set down some of the major components of a decision to build a micro-brewery. This is only a bare outline.

As the Greeks said 2,500 years ago, "Know thyself!" Perhaps the most important question the prospective brewer needs to answer is:

"Why do you want to get into this?" As Alan Davis of Catamount has said: "Is it current job dissatisfaction? A desire to brew the world's best beer? An irresistible entrepreneurial urge? Upon reflection, is it reasonable to expect microbrewing will satisfy these needs? The start-up will be longer and harder than you suspect."*

WHAT TO BREW

The question of what to brew is paradoxically complex. The big difference between the home brewer and the micro-brewer is that, whereas the former makes what he likes, the latter must sell what he makes.

For Professor Michael Lewis it is not enough for a prospective brewer to say, "I want to make a beer *like* Heineken's or Sierra Nevada or Stoudt's Maerzen." The brewer must believe that his is the best possible beer he can produce, for that faith is imperative in elbowing out the dozens of competing brands.

The number of beer styles in this country has exploded in the last ten years. Light lagers were once the overwhelming rule. Today, American micro-brewers (and thousands of home brewers) are making beers in over forty distinct styles. Just a sample includes: brown ale, mead, India pale ale, barley wine, pilsner, porter, bock, Munich, Vienna, steam, rauch, cream ale, herb beer, and alt.

Some of the reasons the micro-brewing pioneers chose ales, porters, and stouts over the more complex lagers were pragmatic. They are not as expensive to make, yet can command import prices. The ale family of beers also matures faster, and at higher temperatures, thus obviating the need for more expensive refrigeration and aging equipment. Finally, the stronger taste of darker beer can cover slight off-flavors; with a light lager, there is no place to hide the mistakes.

In the early days, some micro-brewers could not afford to filter their beer, so they made a virtue out of necessity by asserting that the yeast layer in the bottom and the cloudiness of the brew were marks of "unpasteurized" distinction. There were two problems with this approach. First, Americans drink with their eyes as well as their mouths, and they want

* *American Brewer*, Spring 1992, p. 29.

a clear beer. Second, and more important, living beer is unstable and very susceptible to contamination. Pasteurization didn't become popular to kill taste but to kill infection.

Today, any micro-brewery worth its hops will offer four to eight or more beers during the year. Usually, they will have two or three year-round brews, then brew seasonal or specialty beers—for example, Christmas ales, or bocks. To the yin of the vast expansion in beer styles is joined the yang of increased consumer sophistication and demand. As styles multiply, brewery and brewpub offerings multiply.

The brewpub owner has more flexibility than the micro-brewer. He can experiment with small batches of new beers. If they are popular, he can quickly brew more. If they bomb, he can try something else and change the menu. The micro-brewer has the complex task of producing labels, devising a marketing strategy, and building brand/style loyalty.

HOW TO BREW

There are three choices here: micro-brewery, brewpub, or contract brewing. Each has its pros and cons.

The first option is to follow in the path of Maytag, McAuliffe, Newman, Mason, and Widmer: the free-standing brewery producing beer in bottles and/or kegs. (See cost estimates below.) Obviously, you are driven by your market. You have to get the beer out into a multitude of outlets, both saloons and package stores. There is a higher markup on bottles than on kegs. But bottles require bottler/labelers, which are expensive, hard to find, and often hard to maintain. Packaging is another expense that many prospective brewers fail to consider.

Kegs have their own drawbacks. Name recognition is harder to develop. Getting bars to try a new draft beer is more difficult than trying a new bottle. Keeping track of and cleaning the kegs can be a headache. William Newman launched his Albany Amber on an all-kegs premise, only to find, after a year, that he needed the higher profit margins of bottles. (Yet the Widmer breweries in Oregon have surpassed 30,000 barrels' annual sales of kegs only. It can be done, but it probably takes a special market like Portland's, where micro-brewed beers have surpassed imports in market share.)

The second option for the brewer-to-be is to run a brewpub—i.e., be a restaurateur as well. In this environment, the brewer creates relatively small quantities of beer and sells it in kegs or right from serving tanks. The fact is, if the brewery is a genuine operation (and not a front for contracted beer shipped in), then the owner must worry about two distinct businesses. Under Montana law, for example, this is easier, because that state requires a literal and corporate wall between the brewery and the pub. Juergen Knoeller owns the Bayern Brewery in Missoula, Montana, and sells his beer thirty feet away, at the Iron Horse Brew Pub, which his wife owns.

The advantages of a brewpub over a brewery are several. The profit margins on brewpub beer are three or four times what they are on bottled beer. There are no distribution problems. It's hard to imagine fresher beer than that coming straight out of the storage tanks. Further, the pub brewer has more flexibility in brewing styles. He can make specialty beers almost on demand. All he has to do is change the menu to include a new "Smoked Porter" or Dogbolt Bitter, or Berliner Weisse (to name some of Greg Noonan's offerings). If one style doesn't sell, he quickly shifts to another.

However, there are drawbacks, too. "Not everyone can run a pub," observes Knoeller. "You can't just open it up and expect people to come. You've got to know how to make people feel comfortable. My wife has worked in bars for thirteen or fourteen years. She *knows* how to run a pub. I don't. We have a very lucky combination of skills."

R. C. Schmidt, president of the Water Street Brewery in Milwaukee, agrees that you need both skills. "The brewery is the theater of the brewpub—the attraction. But it takes knowledge of the restaurant business and an equal emphasis on food and service to make [a brewpub] successful."

During the early 1990s, the number of brewpubs launched was double that of the micro-breweries. Charlie Papazian of the Association of Brewers thinks the ratio will continue to widen. The economics of scale are such that the brewpub can be sized to fit the ambitions of the owner and the demands of the restaurant. Conversely, there is probably a limit on the number of local or regional breweries.

The third approach is contract brewing. It was Matthew Reich who pioneered this approach, with his New Amsterdam Ale. Contracting means that you hire an existing brewery, usually an established regional operation with excess capacity, to brew your beers, for which you pay somewhere between $6 and $13 per case, depending upon the batch size. You are then free to concentrate on marketing, distribution, and promotion. If the beer bombs, you are only out the cost of the beer, not an entire brewery.

The person who rewrote the book on contracting was the outspoken James Koch of Boston Brewing Company. In seven years, his Samuel Adams brands grew to almost 400,000 barrels annually, or almost one in four of all the craft beer barrels sold in the U.S. Koch is a phenomenal marketer. He scoffed at those who doted on having their own brew kettles and tanks. He called it "[an] edifice complex. From the business standpoint, it makes no sense to build a brewery. The beer is not going to be cheaper and it's not going to be better."

Several small breweries which bottle their own beer have contracted with larger breweries to fill spikes in demand. Others have contracted out their beers. At least one brewpub, Spanish Peaks in Bozeman, Montana, has contracted with August Schell to brew and bottle its flagship Black Dog Ale, which is kegged for local consumption in Montana. William Newman has turned to Catamount to brew his Saratoga brand. One special case is Brandevor of Seattle, Washington. This company produces house-label brews for several restaurant and hotel chains, such as TGI Friday's Inc. and Marriott Corporation. The company produces four basic kinds of beer, from "light to intense," according to the president, Robert Imeson. In all, about sixty brewing companies contract out their beer.

WHERE TO LEARN BREWING

Micro-brewers have taken several paths to brewing competence. Some, like McAuliffe at New Albion, taught themselves through experience and books. Others, like William Newman of Albany and Steve Mason of Catamount, served apprenticeships at English breweries. Scores of future brewers worked at other micro-breweries or brewpubs. "Not a week goes by that someone doesn't come in or call and ask to work here, even for free, just to get the experience," said Mason. Some brewer-teachers make the students sign an agreement not to open a brewery within a certain distance of their own operations.

Formal courses in brewing and fermentation science are available at two institutions of higher learning. The Siebel Institute of Technology, in Chicago, offers sessions of from three days to ten weeks on Microbrewery and Pub Operations, Sensory Evaluation of Beer, and Brewing Science and Technology. At the University of California at Davis, Michael Lewis's Department of Fermentation Science gives courses and a degree.

I would recommend joining the Institute of Brewing Studies. They offer an array of publications, such as collected transcripts of micro-brewing conferences, *The Brewery Planner: A Guide to Opening Your Own Small Brewery*, brewing textbooks, a list of brewers for hire, and much more. This organization has been at the vortex of the micro-brewing revolution, and its whole *raison d'être* is to help create more successful craft breweries.

SKILLS

At its simplest, Jack McAuliffe said, brewing means turning water into money. However, there is far more to the business than that, and the skills required to succeed are commensurately more numerous. The brewer who starts from scratch must be a hybrid of pack rat, junk dealer, shade-tree mechanic, and surgeon who slavers over food-equipment magazines the way others do over *Playboy*. When asked what kinds of skills the prospective brewer needs, Jim Schleuter of River City said, "Electrical work, plumbing, welding, tile work, carpentry, refrigeration, practical biology, mechanical ability, and all-purpose cussing. Much of it must be in the blood. By the time you're an adult, you don't have time to learn all these things." At the same time, it helps to have what Paul Camusi of Sierra Nevada calls "that indefinable feel for brewing." Some people are born cooks while others, no matter how many cooking courses they take, have tin tongues.

Making good, even excellent beer is only the beginning. You need to line up the financing, market the beer, hold your costs in line with your income, keep your employees productive and happy, etc., etc. In short, you need all the skills required of any successful small business. In the early days of the micro-brewing revolution, a number of brewers were so in love with their beers, they assumed they would sell themselves. Realism has settled in, and brewers are more likely to talk about "the product" than "my beer."

COSTS

How much will the brewery cost? That depends on a host of factors. How much beer do you expect to sell? How much used equipment can you find? Will you make ales or lagers? (How you answer that question alone could change your overall costs by 30 percent.) How much will you pay yourself (and your help)? How much will you pay for rent, utilities, etc.? Will it be a brewpub or a brewery?

Newman and Reich each raised an initial $250,000, but they spent it in dramatically different ways. Newman channeled his money into a building and brewing equipment, whereas Reich put every extra cent over the cost of his contract with F. X. Matt into marketing.

Some prospective brewers think that, with the closing of over seven hundred American breweries in the last forty years, used equipment at 10 cents on the dollar would litter the landscape. Perhaps this was true twenty-five years ago, but today many defunct breweries have been bought and brokered and are pumping beer for Brazilians, Nigerians, and other Third World imbibers.

As the American micro-brewing industry matures, it *has* spun off some usable equipment. Lawrence Miller, founder of Otter Creek Brewing Company in Middlebury, Vermont, bought an entire brewhouse (the major brewing vessels) from Widmer Brewing Company in Portland, Oregon, because Widmer was doubling its capacity with new equipment.

To give a *rough* idea of how much a four-to-six-thousand-barrel freestanding brewery would cost in 1994, I turned to Miller of Otter Creek. Although he assembled his brewery for considerably less, he estimated the costs at $300,000–400,000. If you sell what you make, you will earn a living wage, at least initially.

Start-up Costs

Equipment	$251,000
Leasehold improvement	15,000
Installation	50,000
License & permits	7,000
Deposit/utilities	1,000
Deposit/phone	300
Deposit/rent	2,000
Operating capital	50,000
TOTAL	**$376,300**

The equipment costs broke down as follows:

Malt-handling	$12,000
Spent grains	1,000
Mash-lauter tun	14,000
Hot-water tanks	8,000
Brew kettle (20 barrels)	20,000
Fermenters (5)	70,000
Refrigeration capacity	20,000
Wort chiller	8,000
Beer hose	3,000
Filter unit	10,000
Boiler unit	10,000
Beer barrels (1,000)	55,000
Barrel washer	5,000
One-arm racker	5,000
Lab & cleaning equipment	10,000
TOTAL	**$251,000**

Note that this does not include a bottling line—which could add anywhere from $50,000 to $200,000—or real-estate/rental costs.

It goes without saying that knowing how much the brewery will cost does not guarantee that you can raise the money. You need a financing and ownership structure that will satisfy your backers and bankers.

MARKETING/PRICING

After spending several years developing beer formulas, raising money, finding a location, scrounging for equipment, and living on macaroni and cheese, the new brewer might be forgiven for believing that the beer will be an instant success . . . without marketing. Just a few newspaper articles, a television spot, word of mouth among the local home brewers, and—presto!—the newest kid on the block whips all comers. Alas, the real street corners of the market are far less hospitable or benevolent.

Too many of the early micro-brewers either didn't allocate money for marketing or expected the beer to create its own demand. Today, with hundreds of craft and imported beer "products" on the market, it is imperative for the brewer to find or build a niche with intelligent marketing. As has been said for all sorts of products besides beer, the real competition is anything chosen in preference to your own product.

"There's a big market based on snobbishness out there," observed Michael Lewis. "These craft beers represent the same image as BMW cars, alligator shirts, and Perrier. It's not a fickle market as long as people think they are getting their money's worth. The alligator shirt happens to be an extraordinarily hard-wearing shirt. People are not fools. If they pay $1.50 for a bottle of Sierra Nevada Pale Ale and it's very good, they will say, 'I know something. I'm getting a real gourmet kick for my money.' If the beer is less good, then that customer will drink something else. A lot of hopeful brewers don't understand this—they think they only need to make something a bit better than Budweiser."

"You can't be just a beer geek," said Mark Taverniti, the forthright owner of Spanish Peaks Brewery in Bozeman, Montana. With a background in restaurants, wine, and art, Taverniti saw beer from a marketing perspective. He took some courses at the University of California at Davis "to evaluate the industry. I didn't see many people who approached brewing from the marketing perspective." Taverniti's aim was to use the Bozeman brewery to develop beers for a national market. His first entry was Black Dog Ale, which he hoped would be the next Pete's Wicked Ale. He spent as much time on the label and the image as upon the beer itself. "I want people to buy the beer with the black dog on the label. Clarity in packaging is vital. Everything we do is meant to trigger the memory of that name."

How the beer is priced is almost as important as how it's marketing. Listen to Carol Stoudt, president of Stoudt Brewing Company in Adamstown, Pennsylvania. Specializing in German-style lagers, Stoudt has won a total of twelve medals at three Great American Beer Festivals, including seven golds. She advises the prospective brewer to stay small, become a distinctive local beer with a loyal following—but to sell the beer for what it's worth. "We can't afford to compete even with Pete's, let alone the giant American brewers, because then it's a price game with pallets on the store floor, and we would get killed in no time. My biggest shock when we started to sell off-premises was to find retailers who thought we would give it away. We can't do that. Nor should we try."

DISTRIBUTION

Once the beer is bottled or kegged and sitting on the loading dock, how will you get it to the retailer? After the repeal of Prohibition and the end of brewery-owned bars in the United States, there developed the so-called three-tier system of brewer-distributor-retailer. Distributors handle a range of beverages and even several beers simultaneously. Getting one of them to take on a micro-brewed product requires some convincing.

In the early days of the micro-brewing revolution, some brewers opted for self-distribution, where permissible. This made sense for developing good rapport with retail accounts, but it was impractical when distribution expanded beyond a local market. Other micro-brewers hooked up with distributors specializing in imported beers.

Today, it is paradoxically both easier and harder for a micro-brewery to get distributed. Through the meteoric success of Samuel Adams and smaller breweries, distributors now know about the craft brewing market segment. At the same time, with so many new breweries clamoring for attention, the distributors can pick and choose their accounts.

"If you want to be a market force," cautions Lawrence Miller, "you need to have someone else distribute for you."

REGULATIONS

Beer is a regulated drug. Like it or not, when you make and distribute beer, federal, state, and local officials have a special interest in you and your work. If you don't like regulations and rules, you probably shouldn't be brewing for a living.

The federal Alcohol, Tobacco, and Firearms Bureau is primarily interested in your criminal record—if you are a convicted felon, you may not brew—and your readiness to pay a $7-per-barrel federal tax.

Every state has its own alcohol regulatory agency. The brewer must also please the state in other matters, such as health and employment codes, manufacturers' fees, etc. Local authorities oversee zoning and building permits.

What follows is a representative list of permits and approvals required before opening:

1. Name permit and publication (also known as "d.b.a.")
2. Environmental impact report
3. Approval of neighboring owners
4. Approval of landlord/owner
5. Building inspection
6. Health inspection
7. Zoning approval

8. Alcoholic beverage manufacturer's license
9. Label approval/recycling compliance
10. Water-resources/town-discharge permit

11. ATF Bureau
    a. Brewer's bond of $1,000
    b. Tax rates
    c. Operational reports
    d. Occupational stamp
    e. Label approval

12. Personal questionnaires going back ten years for you and all employees

13. Employer's ID number from the IRS
14. Incorporation papers

WHERE TO BUILD

Where the brewery is housed is not nearly as important as how the beer is made. Unquestionably, brick holds a powerful attraction, especially if you want the structure to promote a traditional brewing image. Brick conjures up images of sprawling Victorian factories where stout men in mustaches, derbies, and suspenders made real beer. At least, that was *my* dream as I, in my early romantic phase, drove around Burlington and adjoining Winooski looking for possible sites. Both cities were in the midst of downtown revitalization, and developers saw money to make in converting abandoned brick fabric mills. The most picturesque location nearby was at Shelburne Farms, a thousand-acre remnant of a Victorian estate on Lake Champlain. One of the remaining buildings, the Farm Barn, was a massive, five-story structure with cupolas, copper roof, and brooding dark shingles. The estate was controlled by a nonprofit corporation dedicated to education and various farm ventures, such as dairying and cheesemaking. Given their hundreds of acres of field to plant with barley and perhaps hops, such self-sufficiency, coupled with the building, would make an irresistibly great marketing ploy.

When I went to the manager with my half-serious plan, he gave me a curious look and said, "This is the second time in six months I've been approached with that same idea." The other proposal had come from two Germans who said they wanted to bring a German brewhouse to Shelburne, grow their own barley and hops, produce about 50,000 barrels annually, and capture 10 percent of the Vermont beer market. (This was at a time when Molson, after ten years of hard selling, still had less than a 5-percent share.) If these guys were serious, this was hardball, not slow-pitch softball. I couldn't play in that league.

As it turned out, the Shelburne Farms brewery was stillborn. A falling-out between the partners sent the brewmaster back to Germany. Meanwhile, I had come to my senses. I asked myself some of those basic questions. Did I really want to be a commercial brewer and devote a hundred hours a week to the task, as Greg Noonan was doing with his brewpub? Did I have the technical and managerial skills to oversee construction and operation? Did I have the marketing, money, and moxie to sell my beer?

In the end, I realized I had no more business in commercial brewing than I had in professional bagpiping, or full-time beekeeping, or running marathons every couple of weeks. I didn't think I could raise the $500,000 for a real try at success. I was pretty sure I didn't have the mechanical skills to run pumps and bottling lines. I was probably not conscientious enough to maintain the operating-room cleanliness needed to make uncontaminated beer month after month.

The words of Michael Lewis came back to me: "The ones who make it in this business will be extreme characters. The work is extraordinarily hard, and those that don't give it one hundred percent won't get to first base. This is a seven-day job if you build from scratch. To be successful, the micro-brewer must have a *savage commitment* to every aspect of brewing and selling. For every hundred people who think about building a brewery, ten may try it and only one will succeed."

Finally, as Fritz Maytag warned, "To be a brewer, you must have nightmares regularly. You've got to think about problems all the time."

By this time I knew I wasn't prepared for that kind of devotion, that amount of work, or that little sleep. For me it was home to home brew.

The Brewing Capital of the World ("Think Globally; Drink Locally")

The decision not to build a brewery surely simplified my life and allowed me to take uncomplicated pleasure in the hobby of home brewing. True, I was using more complex equipment—wort chiller, propane stove, and kegs—and brewing more elaborate beers. But brewing was again a comfortable, predictable, manageable pursuit, which left time for my other hobbies of beekeeping, running, fly-fishing, and . . . my family. Like the farmer adjusting to the seasons, I could brew six to eight times a year, drink one or two glasses of an evening, and give the rest away.

Of course, my beers tasted better than those of the mega-brewers. They also tasted better than most of the imported beers, because I had them beat on freshness. However, I couldn't match most of the domestic craft brews. Should I weep? Not at all. "Losing" to these beers gave me the same pleasure I had when our older son first beat me in tennis: it was the sweetest of defeats.

To build a commercial brewery is the fantasy of every serious home brewer. But I don't have to fulfill this dream. Interestingly, it was a passage from a book on another hobby—fishing—that put this avocation-vocation tension into perspective. In *The Philosophical Fisherman*, Harold Blaisdell described a pastime with all the fun squeezed out of it:

A man can be so caught up in fishing that it actually becomes a grim business, and when this happens, it is time to slow the tempo and take a breather. It is time . . . to shift his attention from the fish and focus it upon himself. If a fellow can do this, if he can sit quietly for a day and do nothing more pretentious than keep half an eye on a bobber or the tip of his rod, he will see many things he has been missing. . . . If he obtains the proper state of objectivity, he will see in himself all the ludicrous qualities which make him the human being he is.

By sticking to *home* brewing, I can still rejoice in the many-splendored brewing revolution that has washed across the United States. After all, I've been a bit player in this great movement. I've helped found a brewing club. I've contributed a book on the subject. I've helped to legalize brewpubs in Vermont.

As I look back on the last ten to fifteen years, I see members of a disparate orchestra assembling to produce music for the palate. Their simple theme, which they built into exceedingly complex fugues and variations, was the production of excellent beer. Beer styles are like concertos and string quartets. Brewers are both composers and performers as they present their offerings. Some play for their own benefit, others play for their friends, and some even charge money.

The first scratching of this music sounded over twenty years ago, as a result of the growing disaffection from the monotonous, light American lager beer and primitive brewing ingredients. When I started brewing in the early 1970s, Prohibition-era methods and ingredients were the rule. A few lucky guerrilla brewers had access to English malts and hops. For the rest of us, Blue Ribbon hopped malt syrup, cane sugar, and baker's yeast were the Hobson's choices. It was like being asked to play Paganini on a washtub fiddle.

Today, the home brewer is awash in varieties of malt, hops, and yeast. Further, there seems no limit to the equipment improvements some brewers demand (and suppliers offer). There are now manufacturers who offer complete stainless-steel "pilot" brewhouses to the home brewer for $800–1,200. It is no wonder that many micro-brewers still come out of the home brewer ranks. The influence flows in reverse as well. Home brewers discover particular craft beers they like. The next thing they do is run down to the local retailer to demand supplies and equipment to play the same beery melodies.

Thus, "symbiotic" is a word several professional brewers use to describe the relationship between their fraternity and home brewers. "Both belong to the same beer culture that's concerned with careful production of high-quality products, with drawing the best of taste and color and balance from their beers," said Steve Mason of Catamount Brewing. Home brewers become some of the most loyal (and sometimes critical) customers of the local brewery. They are never numerous enough to assure brewery profitability, but they do become almost as proprietary as baseball or hockey fans. Most professional brewers are grateful and responsive. Greg Noonan, owner of the Vermont Pub and Brewery, and himself a former home brewer, helped launch the Green Mountain Mashers home brewing club. He shares his technical skills with them, and recently he went further. At the Vermont State Home Brew Competition, which had almost three hundred entries, he agreed to brew one of the style winners. He and his head brewer tasted the best beers in each of twelve categories and chose a brown ale to brew for sale in his pub.

Think of the beer styles explosion as another instrument in the symphony of good beer. Over several post-Prohibition decades, the American public was conditioned to drinking one style, a light American lager. To resurrect and develop other beer styles was one of the early educational goals of the American Homebrewers Association. Brewing different styles of beer would not only reveal the breadth of malted beverages, it would also stimulate the innovative and competitive juices among home brewers. Papazian and his AHA music teachers knew they could not simply announce that Dopplebock, Amber, Pilsner, Brown Ale, etc., were the acceptable styles. That would be to hold a concert without an audience. So they began to sponsor competitions in which people could submit their beers. As the competitions caught on and the entrants multiplied, they realized their judging techniques were too capricious and idiosyncratic. Thus, the AHA, together with the Home Wine and Beer Trade Association, developed a Beer Judge Certification Program. The program has the dual purpose of ensuring judging consistency and giving brewers constructive criticism on their beers. The prospective judges are tested on topics such as brewing techniques, grains, hops, water, brewing history, and beer styles. After passing the initial test, these judges can reach five levels of expertise, based upon "experience points" earned by judging local, regional, and national competitions. As a result, scores of local and regional competitions were launched, including the "World Series" of home brew contests, the annual AHA National Competition.

What's more, home brewers who turned professional added to the chorus of beer style entrepreneurs. With the broad acceptance of more than two score beer styles, the American beer drinker has, as one home brewer calls it, a "symphony of suds" from which to choose. Three quick examples will show this variety. Samuel Adams/Boston Beer Company offers ten to twelve different styles of beer to a national market. In Brattleboro, Vermont, former cellist and current brewer Ray McNeill has twelve of his own beers on tap, ranging from lightest lager to darkest stout. At the Spanish Peaks brewpub in Bozeman, Montana, a wheat beer is offered as the introductory beverage.

As of 1993, there were over four hundred "craft brewing companies" (micros, brewpubs, contract brewers, and regional brewers) in the United States, producing over 1.5 million barrels of beer, up 2,000 percent in ten years. (There were ten such breweries ten years before.) In at least one market (Portland, Oregon), domestic craft beers outsold imports. Breweries and brewpubs were springing up every month. Tiny Vermont, with only 600,000 residents, had four brewpubs and three micro-breweries. Most observers felt that the number of brewpubs would double or triple that of micro-breweries, because of the ease of entry, the cost of a bottling line, and the higher profitability of brewpub beer.

Some craft brewers predict that their market segment will rise to 5 percent (overall U.S. beer production in 1992 was 182 million barrels). German-born and -trained brewer Juergen Knoeller of Missoula's Bayern Brewery even foresees that in ten years the domestic craft beers will largely displace the imports, because they are just as well made, fresher, and cheaper.

Tom Burns of Detroit and Mackinac Brewing Company is more skeptical. "People will still buy mainstream imports who have big marketing bucks, like Heineken's, the Canadian beers, Guinness, and Bass. There will always be a demand for high-quality European beers, but the micros will make a big dent." Samuel Adams founder Jim Koch is even more cautious. "If we are all very fortunate (meaning the small brewers), maybe five percent of beer drinkers will drink this kind of beer half the time. If we are fortunate, craft-brewed beers will reach one to two percent of the total beer market. . . . I'd love to see the rest of the world look like the Portland or Seattle markets, but somehow I just don't think it's going to happen."

One interesting sidelight of these developments is that the craft brewers no longer publicly denounce the mega-brewers. Between the two there has grown up a degree of mutual respect. The micro-brewers acknowledge the technical and marketing skills of the giants, and the giants appreciate the dedication and flexibility of the craft brewers. Further, the craft brewers realize that their competition is the imports, not Miller and Bud. Finally, when it comes to the threat of higher excise taxes, *all* brewers feel the impact of Washington.

Since I was so wrong ten years ago, I hesitate to predict the future of brewing in America. I would rather present my hopes and educated guesses. I like Carol Stoudt's dream.

"My hope is that the people who get into the industry, who really love the beer, will try to create a beer that is unique to that area, instead of just making a Sunoco blend of beer that could be sold anywhere. Their market area should be within a short drive of the brewery, so that people can come to the brewery, identify with it, and buy beer there possibly. The brewery will become part of the landscape, like a favorite park, or statue, or restaurant. We are taking people who drink Michelob and Killian's Red, and we're taking them to fresh beer and great styles. The only way we can do that is to stay local.

"You have to be a certain size, but then you don't have to compromise. Be modest, keep product quality up. Don't ever try to compete with the big guys, because then it's a price game and you get killed."

Greg Noonan of the Vermont Pub and Brewery echoes this sentiment. "The breweries that establish a strong regional or local identity will survive. That means, however, that the brewers will make solid products. Today, the consumer is more sophisticated about craft beers and also less tolerant of off-flavors. You can't get away with things you did five years ago. Furthermore, with a host of products to choose from, *you* must give the customer a reason for buying *your* beer. Brand or style loyalty will go only to those who deserve it."

When you put all these factors together—increased numbers of brewers and breweries, improvements in ingredients, more sophisticated and discriminating tastes, and broad acceptance of brewing styles— you have a recipe for the United States' becoming, in Charlie Papazian's phrase, *"the beer capital of the world.* If people are real beer lovers, they will come to this country. We'll never have the history and tradition of specific styles that Germany and Belgium and England have. But we will have the greatest beer diversity."

Papazian's remarks tie in closely with Pat Baker's observation that the U.S. bids fair to being the most "beer literate" nation in our appreciation of diverse beer styles. Home brewers and micro-brewers are constantly experimenting. As they explore new styles, they are further educating the American public.

As home brewers and micro-brewers continue to innovate, the whole notion of brand loyalty has changed, observes Tom Burns. Instead of choosing one beer for all occasions—one size fits all—a beer drinker might have four, six, or ten different beers. As befits one whose brewery is blocks from Detroit's Tiger Stadium, Burns uses a baseball metaphor. "The quality beer drinker has a rotation. He might have a Sam Adams, then an Anchor. His lawnmower beer might be Molson. Then he would drink mine. Then go to a Bass. Then he comes back and starts again. As long as I'm in the rotation, I'm happy."

The home brewer has the same rotation, with the difference that he makes most of it himself. In the last ten years, the American Homebrewers Association's membership has grown fivefold—to 20,000. No one keeps statistics on the numbers of brewers overall. Maybe it's 500,000, as Pat Baker believes, or 1 million, as Charlie Papazian thinks. I would buy either number. These are people who brew for the quality, not the quantity or the price advantage. (However, if the federal government boosts the excise tax on a six-pack of beer by $1 or $2 to help underwrite universal health insurance, the number of home brewers could soar.)

Of those who brew, most will remain extract brewers. Time is the biggest factor. Few brewers want to spend seven to nine hours making two cases of beer. Also, all-grain brewing does require more complex and expensive equipment. On the positive side, the improvements in ingredients and techniques (including specialty grains) have made extract so good that some such brewers have won national awards.

Brewing offers creativity, the pleasure of sharing, competition, technological intrigue, practical dreams, a pleasant high, variety, literary license.

Home brewing is very much like cooking in its practice and its rewards. The ambitious cook is driven by a mixture of discipline, order, freedom, and pride; the same is true of the serious brewer. We use other people's recipes as training ropes before cutting free to find our own paths.

Home brewing will continue to attract the same kind of people who belong to our club—individuals with adventuresome palates and hands, and probably the funds to buy imported beers, but the curiosity, pride, and innovativeness to make their own Guinness or Chimay or Dortmunder. Any home brewer now has the means to match almost any brand of commercial beer, provided he assigns some value to his emotional involvement. All home brewers are missionaries, and, as one, I hope that all serious beer drinkers will try to brew their own at least once. Many will be intrigued and continue.

Fully as important as pleasing yourself, the joy of home brewing lies in pleasing others. Some are ordinary beer drinkers who might nurse a bottle of Heineken's for an hour but like the taste. Others are brewers themselves. Others are just friends.

In this book I have celebrated home brewing and micro- or craft brewing. Its practitioners belong to a ten-thousand-year-old tradition that includes Sumerian peasants, German braumeisters, English brewsters, George Washington, and H. L. Mencken. Beer was once one of the world's great folk beverages. Only during the last few decades did it become the bland, monotonous, highly carbonated drink most people leaned into at a bar or bought as an afterthought in a grocery store. Thanks to the efforts of people like Fred Eckhardt, Charlie Papazian, Fritz Maytag, and Carol Stoudt, and hundreds of thousands of home brewers, a "concord of sweet sounds" rings again, to use Shakespeare's phrase. Through their diligent and creative efforts, they have helped to restore beer to its proper place as a great food and art form.

Making your own beer is full of paradoxes. To "have a beer" is synonymous with relaxing, yet brewing is a matter of hard work and concentration. Beer is the surpassing drink of companionship and conviviality, yet it is best made in solitude. You brew to suit your own taste, yet your greatest satisfaction probably comes in sharing it with others. The more you make, the more you pause to savor each sip and swallow.

Home brew has decisively shed its image of an explosive harking back to Prohibition. Modern home brew is as different from its Prohibition-era ancestor as Beefeaters is from bathtub gin. Moreover, the average home brewer has an immense variety of beers to make. Just as there is a wine for every mood and occasion, so there is a beer. Shouldn't that beer be the tastiest, most delicious, most lovingly crafted beer around—*your* home brew?

Cheers!

Appendixes

Appendix I: Recipes

Home Brewing Is a Metaphor for Life Ale (India Pale Ale)

5 gals. water
2 tsps. gypsum
6–7 lbs. amber malt extract, liquid or dried
⅔ cups malt extract (priming)
1½–2 oz. Northern Brewer pellets (boiling) 14–20
2 packets top-fermenting yeast
1 tsp. Irish Moss
1 oz. Cascade hops (aromatic) pellets

Boil 2 gals. water. Add gypsum. Turn off heat. Add malts.

Boil 20 minutes. Add half the bittering (Northern Brewer) hops.

Withdraw 1 cup wort. Force-cool to 75° F., and add 2 packets yeast to make yeast starter. Cover.

Boil wort 20 minutes, add rest of bittering hops and Irish Moss, and boil 20 minutes more. Turn off heat. Add aromatic hops. Stir.

Put 3 gals. of cool water in clean carboy. Siphon wort into carboy. Top up to make five gals. If temperature is below 75° F., add yeast starter, attach blow-by tube.

When primary fermentation is complete, attach fermentation lock and let brew ferment flat.

Bottle with ⅔ cup dried malt extract (or dextrose) dissolved in hot water. Age 3–5 weeks.

NOTE: Yeast sediment is a fact of life for home brew. It is good for you, being laced with B vitamins, but it will cloud the beer if the bottle is shaken. Therefore, if you want to drink clear beer, you must pour it carefully, all at one time. To leave the sediment in the bottle, incline the (uncapped) bottle so that the beer flows into the tilted mug or glass. Stop when the sediment approaches the spout.

If you don't care about clarity, and want a bigger dose of B vitamins, just pour the entire contents, sediment and all.

Sap Beer

4 lbs. dried malt extract, light or dark
1 pint maple syrup
5 gals. water
1 tsp. Irish Moss
2 oz. Willamette hops, of which ½ oz. is for aroma
2 packets top-fermenting yeast

This is a variation on a colonial recipe that used maple sap as the basic ingredient for beer.

Follow the directions for the HBIAMFL Ale above. The great difference in this beer is its taste. If you have ever boiled your own maple syrup and burned some of it in the pan, this beer will remind you of that luscious smoky flavor.

Ma Vlast Lager

10 lbs. pale six-row malt
2 oz. Saaz (or comparable) hops 10–13 HBU bittering
½ to ¾ oz. Saaz aromatic hops 2–3 HBU

3 tsps. gypsum
1 tsp. Irish Moss
½ cup dried malt extract for priming
1 packet Wyeast Bohemian yeast, built to 1 pint starter

For procedures, read Chapter 8.

Original gravity: 1.045–1.050
Final gravity: 1.012–1.018

Boneshaker Porter

10 lbs. of two-row pale malt
1½ oz. Eroica, or Galena hops bittering
1 lb. crushed crystal malt
4 oz. chocolate malt
4 oz. flaked barley
4 oz. black malt
1 tsp. Irish Moss
1 oz. Tettnanger (or Cascade) aromatic hops
1 tsp. gypsum
1 packet Wyeast London yeast built to 1 pint starter

Add gypsum to 2½ gal. water.
Mash pale malt at between 150° F. and 155° F. two hours.
Sparge at 170° F. to recover 6½ gal. of wort.
Boil for 90 minutes, adding half an ounce of bittering hops every 30 minutes.
Add specialty malts after 30 minutes, loose or in a cloth bag. After 60 minutes, add Irish Moss.
After 90 minutes, turn off heat, wait 5 minutes. Stir in the aromatic hops. Wait 5 minutes.

Cool, with wort chiller if possible.
Transfer to primary fermenter with yeast starter.

When primary fermentation is complete (4–5 days), transfer to secondary fermenter.

Fermentation should conclude in 2–3 weeks.

Bottle or keg, wait 2–3 weeks, and enjoy.

Original gravity: 1.055–1.060
Final gravity: 1.015–1.025

Appendix II: Brewing Suppliers, Breweries/Brewpubs, and Brews

SELECTED BREWING SUPPLIERS

Alternative Beverage
114 Freeland Lane, Suite O
Charlotte, NC 28217
(800) 365-BREW

Bacchus & Barleycorn, Ltd.
8725Z Johnson Dr.
Merriam, KS 66202
(913) 262-4243

Barleymalt & Vine
26 Elliot St.
Newton, MA 02161
(800) 666-7026

The Beverage People
840 Piner R. #14
Santa Rosa, CA 95403
(800) 544-1867

Chicago Indoor Garden Supply
297 N. Barrington Rd.
Streamwood, IL 60107
(800) 444-2837

DeFalco's Home Wine & Beer
  Supplies
5611 Morningside Dr. Dept. Z
Houston, TX 77005
(713) 523-8154

Something's Brewing
196 Battery St.
Durlington, VT 05401
(802) 660-9007

Vermont Homebrewer's Supply
20 Susie Wilson Rd.
Essex, VT 05451
(800) 456-BREW

William's Brewing
Box 2195-Y9
San Leandro, CA 94577
(800) 759-6025

SELECTED BREWERIES AND BREWPUBS
IN THE UNITED STATES

Anchor Brewing Co.
San Francisco, CA

Buffalo Bill's Brewery
Hayward, CA

Mendocino Brewing Co.
Hopland, CA

Sierra Nevada Brewing Co.
Chico, CA

Goose Is. Brewing Co.
Chicago, IL

Oldenberg Brewery
Ft. Mitchell, KY

Abita Brewing Co.
Abita Springs, LA

D. L. Geary Brewing Co.
Portland, ME

Boston Brewing Co.
Boston, MA

Cambridge Brewing Co.
Cambridge, MA

St. Louis Brewery
St. Louis, MO

Bayern Brewing Co.
Missoula, MT

Spanish Peaks Brewing Co.
Bozeman, MT

Woodstock Brewing Co.
Kingston, NY

McMenamin's Brew Pubs
Portland, OR area

Widmer Brewing Co.
Portland, OR

Stoudt Brewery
Adamstown, PA

Old Dominion Brewing Co.
Ashburn, VA

Catamount Brewing Co.
White River Jct., VT

McNeill's Brewery
Brattleboro, VT

Otter Creek Brewing Co.
Middlebury, VT

Vermont Pub & Brewery
Burlington, VT

Sprecher Brewing Co.
Milwaukee, WI

Pyramid Ales
Kalama, WA

Redhook Ale Brewery
Seattle, WA

Yakima Brewing Co.
Yakima, WA

MY FAVORITE AMERICAN CRAFT BEERS
(a very subjective—and very incomplete—list)

Anchor Steam Beer

Catamount Amber

Grant's Imperial Stout

Samuel Adams Double Bock

Sierra Nevada Pale Ale

Stoudt's Pilsner

Glossary

Adjuncts. Unmalted cereal grain or fermentable ingredients added to malted barley during mashing to produce more, and usually cheaper, sugars. Common adjuncts are rice, corn, wheat.

Aging. Or maturation, during which time the yeast drops out of the beer and the flavor changes to make beer smooth and mellow.

Alcohol. In beer is ethyl alcohol (C_2H_5OH), the preservative and intoxicating component in fermented beverages. Roughly half of the product of fermentation.

Ale. A beer brewed with top-fermenting yeast at warmer temperatures (60°–70° F.) Usually, but not always, a faster maturing beer.

All-grain beer. A beer made entirely from malted barley, as opposed to one made with either all-malt extract or a combination of the two.

Ascorbic acid. Good for colds, good as anti-oxidant in beer. Added just before bottling.

Bacteria. A group of micro-organisms which reproduce rapidly. Unfriendly to beer. Acetobacter and lactobacillus are two particularly bad chaps for brewers.

Barrel. Standard unit of commercial beer production. In the U.S. a barrel equals 31 gallons.

Beer. The generic name for alcoholic beverages produced by fermenting cereal grain or grains.

Black patent. Barley malt that has been kilned at 450° F. to produce a rich, roasted flavor. Generally used in stouts.

Body. A term to describe the fullness of beers, how they feel and taste.

Bottom-fermenting. Describes the type of yeast for making lagers which require colder fermenting temperatures and a slower process.

Brewing. The marriage of malt, hops, and water, through mashing and boiling.

Carbon dioxide. The gas given off during fermentation, roughly equal in weight to the alcohol produced at the same time.

Carboy. Large narrow-necked glass vessel, used as both primary and secondary fermenter.

Chlorine detergent. Powerful sterilant for all bottles and equipment. However, it can kill yeast, so containers and equipment must be well drip-dried or rinsed after using it.

Conditioning. The process of developing carbon dioxide in the beer; enclosed fermentation.

Crystal or caramel malt. Malted barley which has been wetted while sugars are still in the grain, then dried at 250° F. to give a golden color and nutlike flavor to the beer. Used frequently in darker ales.

Diastase. The name for the combination of alpha and beta amylase enzymes that are released from the malt during mashing and that act to convert malt starches to malt sugars, dextrins, and maltose.

Fermentation. The process wherein yeast converts grain sugars into roughly equal parts of carbon dioxide and alcohol.

Fermentation lock. Also known as an air lock or bubbler; water-filled plastic stopper that during fermentation permits carbon dioxide to escape while excluding air (and thus contamination).

Finings. Substances, like gelatin or sturgeon bladder, used to clarify beer during secondary fermentation.

Flocculation. Coalescence and settling of the yeast cells during fermentation and aging, part of the process of clearing the beer.

Gypsum. Calcium sulphate, a salt used to harden water for making pale beers, especially pale ales.

Hops. For brewing purposes, the flowers of the hops plant, *Humulus lupulus*, which provide both bitterness and aroma to the beer. Since the essential oils, which provide the aroma, are lost in boiling, common practice is to add a portion of the "aromatic" hops at the end of the boil. If hops are then added during fermentation, the process is called "dry-hopping."

Hops pellets. Hops flowers that have been pulverized and compressed into pellet-form for convenience and preservation.

Hydrometer. A glass tube with lead or mercury ballast for measuring the specific gravity or density of a liquid compared to pure water. Pure water at 15° C. (59° F.) by definition has a gravity of 1.000. The hydrometer helps the brewer keep track of the progress of fermentation.

Irish Moss. A small amount of this refined seaweed added to the last part of the boil aids in assuring a clear beer.

Kraeusen (pronounced kroy-sen). The first foaming head of beer during fermentation. Also refers to the process of adding some fresh green beer to older aging beer to carbonate the latter naturally.

Lager. Beer fermented at colder temperatures for longer periods of time with a bottom-fermenting yeast. The predominate beer style throughout the world. From the German word *lagern,* "to store."

Light. May refer to body or color of beer. In the United States, "light" is now synonymous with low-calorie beers such as Miller Lite.

Malt extract. A thick, sugary syrup or dry powder prepared from malt. It is simply sweet wort reduced to a syrup or powder by evaporating most of the water.

Malting. The controlled germination of grain by careful steeping and drying to ready malt starches for conversion to sugars.

Mashing. The controlled steeping or soaking of malted barley to release enzymes which convert malt starches to fermentable and nonfermentable sugars.

Nonfermentables. The portion of the malt sugars that will not ferment and therefore add sweetness and body to the beer.

Original gravity. The original specific gravity of beer before fermentation begins. *See* Hydrometer.

pH. Measure of acidity or alkalinity of beer. Acidity increases (pH decreases) from mashing to boiling to fermentation and aging.

Pitching. Adding yeast to cooled wort to begin fermentation.

Porter. A dark, heavy, sweet ale, originally called "entire" because it was drawn from three different gravity taps. A favorite of the porters in London in the early eighteenth century, hence the name.

Potential alcohol. An estimate of the final alcohol content of the brew, based upon the measured sugar content at the beginning of fermentation. In all-malt beers, potential never becomes actual, because of the nonfermentable sugars in solution.

Priming. Adding a small amount of sugar to beer just before bottling to reactivate the yeast and thus carbonate the beverage.

Racking. The process of transferring beer from one vessel to another or into bottles or kegs, while leaving behind the dregs at the bottom of the first container.

Reinheitsgebot. The most important law relating to beer ever passed. The "Purity Law" of Germany, from 1516, decreeing that beer shall consist only of malt, hops, and water (the yeast was assumed).

Sparge. To wash out all soluble products from the mash prior to boiling.

Specific gravity. A measure of the density of a liquid or solid, as compared with that of water, which is conventionally given the value of 1.000. Brewers use gravity to measure the fermentation's progress—the more fermentable sugars, the higher the gravity; the more alcohol, the lower the gravity.

Starter. A strongly fermenting yeast culture that gives a running start to the fermentation of a larger volume of bitter wort.

Steam beer. America's only original beer. Brewed first in ice-less California, steam beer is a lager fermented at ale temperatures. Called "steam" beer because of the lively head caused by kraeusening.

Stout. Dark, robust, full-bodied ale, the most famous exemplar being Guinness.

Top-fermenting. Describes the type of yeast used for ales and stouts, that is, one which works at warmer temperatures and faster speed.

Water treatment. The addition of certain salts, such as gypsum, to harden water for brewing.

Wort (pronounced wert). The liquid solution of malt sugars which forms the basis of beer. Sweet wort precedes the boil and lacks hops; bitter wort includes the hops.

Yeast. The *sine qua non* of beer; the microorganisms that give us bread, wine, and especially beer. In beer, they consume malt sugars and convert them to roughly equal portions of carbon dioxide and ethyl alcohol.

Yeast nutrients. Recommended in recipes where less than half of the sugar comes from malt. Unnecessary with higher proportions of malt because nutrients inhere in malt.

Bibliography

Books

Abel, Bob, *The Book of Beer* (Chicago, Illinois: Henry Regnery, 1976).

American Homebrewers Association, *Microbrewers Resources Directory* (A.H.A., Box 287, Boulder, CO 80306).

Baron, Stanley W., *Brewed in America* (Boston, Massachusetts: Little, Brown, 1962). Reprinted 1972 by Arno Press.

Beach, David, *Homegrown Hops* (Junction City, Oregon, 1992).

Berry, C. J. J., *Home Brewed Beers and Stouts* (Andover, England: Amateur Winemaker Publications Ltd, 1963).

Bravery, H. E., *Home Brewing Without Failures* (New York: Arc Books, 1966).

Briggs, Hough, Stevens, & Young, *Malting and Brewing Science*, 2nd ed. 2 vols. (London, England: Chapman & Hall, 1981).

Brown, Sanborn C., *Wines and Beers of Old New England* (Hanover, New Hampshire: University Press of New England, 1978).

Burch, Byron, *Brewing Quality Beers* (San Rafael, California: Joby Books, 1986).

———, *Quality Brewing* (El Cerrito, California: Joby Books, 441 Lexington Street, CA 94530, 1977).

Coe, Lee, *The Beginner's Home Brew Book* (Portland, Oregon: S. B. Taylor & Assoc., 1972).

Dunn, Michael, *The Penguin Guide to Real Draft Beer* (Middlesex, England: Penguin, 1979).

Eckhardt, Fred, *A Treatise on Lager Beers* (Portland, Oregon: Hobby Winemaker, 2758 N.E. Broadway, OR 97232, 1979).

Forget, Carl, *Dictionary of Beer and Brewing* (Boulder, Colorado: Association of Brewers, 1988).

Foster, Terrence, *Dr. Foster's Book of Beer* (London, England: A & C Black Publishers Ltd, 1979).

Hardman, Michael, and Theo Bergstrom, *Beer Naturally* (London, England: Bergstrom & Boyle Books Ltd, 1976).

Hooker, Richard J., *A History of Food and Drink in America* (Indianapolis, Indiana: Bobbs-Merrill, 1981).

Jackson, Michael, *The Simon and Schuster Pocket Guide to Beer* (New York: Simon and Schuster, 1994).

Johns, Bud, *The Ombibulous Mr. Mencken* (San Francisco, California: Synergistic Press, 1968).

Kramer, Samuel, *The Sumerians* (Chicago, Illinois: University of Chicago Press, 1963).

Lender, Mark E., and James Kirby Martin, *Drinking in America: A History* (New York: Free Press, 1982).

Line, Dave, *The Big Book of Brewing* (Andover, England: Amateur Winemaker Publications Ltd, 1979).

Lundy, Desmond, *A Standard Handbook for the Production of Handmade Beers* (Victoria, British Columbia: Fermenthaus, P.O. Box 4220, V8X 3X8, 1979).

Master Brewers Association, *The Practical Brewer* (Madison, Wisconsin, 1977). This is a professional text, but well written and, for the serious home brewer, well worth having.

Miller, Dave, *Brewing the World's Great Beers* (Pownall, Vermont: Storey Publications, 1988).

———, *The Complete Handbook of Home Brewing* (Pownall, Vermont: Storey Communications, Inc., 1988).

Morison, S. E., *Harvard College in the Seventeenth Century* (Cambridge, Massachusetts: Harvard University Press, 1936).

Morris, Stephen, *The Great Beer Trek* (Brattleboro, Vermont: Stephen Greene Press, 1984).

Noonan, Greg, *Brewing Lager Beer* (Boulder, Colorado: Brewers Publications, 1986).

Orton, Vrest, *The Homemade Beer Book* (Rutland, Vermont: Charles Tuttle, 1973).

Orwell, George, "Hop-Picking" in *An Age Like This*, volume 1 of *The Collected Essays, Journalism and Letters of George Orwell*, ed. Sonia Orwell and Ian Angus (New York: Harcourt, Brace & World, 1968).

Owens, Bill, *How to Build a Small Brewery: Draft Beer in Ten Days* (Ann Arbor, Michigan: G. W. Kent, Inc., 1992).

Papazian, Charlie, *The New Complete Joy of Home Brewing* (New York: Avon Books, 1991).

———, *The Brewer's Companion*, 1994.

Shales, Ken, *Brewing Better Beers* (Andover, England: Amateur Winemaker Publications Ltd, 1967).

For the prospective professional brewer, the Institute of Brewing Studies has developed an extensive library of publications. They include a "Brewery Introduction Packet," micro-brewer's, contract brewer's, and brewpub "starter sets," transcripts of micro-brewing technical conferences, some of the major professional brewing texts, etc. Contact them at Box 1679, Boulder, CO 80306-1679.

Periodicals

American Brewer, Box 510, Hayward, CA 94543. Lively, bimonthly magazine about beer and brewing.

All About Beer, Box 586402, Dept. 8, Oceanside, CA 92058

BEER, The Magazine, Box 717, Hayward, CA 94543-0717

Brewers Digest, 4049 W. Paterson Ave., Chicago, IL 60646.

The New Brewer, bimonthly publication of Institute for Brewing Studies. Box 1679, Boulder, CO 80306-1679; covers the micro-brewing industry.

What's Brewing. Monthly newspaper of Campaign for Real Ale; membership in CAMRA for £5 includes a year's subscription (CAMRA Ltd, 34 Alma Road, St. Albans, Herts AL1 3BW, England).

Zymurgy, quarterly publication of the American Homebrewers Association. Box 1679, Boulder, CO 80306-1679. Covers the home brewing industry and movement. Has extensive list of brewing-related books.

Articles

Davidson, Harold O., "The Bell Doesn't Toll for All Small Brewers," *Beverage World*, March 1981, pp. 29–33.

Eckhardt, Fred, "Talk to Your Beer," *Amateur Brewer Bulletin* No. 9, January 1983.

————, "Hops," *Amateur Brewer Bulletin* No. 4, Fall 1977.

Hartman, Louis F., and A. L. Oppenheim, "On Beer and Brewing Techniques in Ancient Mesopotamia," Supplement to the *Journal of the American Oriental Society*, Number 10 (Baltimore: The American Oriental Society, 1950).

Petri, Bill, "Malting Your Own Barley," *Zymurgy*, Special Issue 1981, p. 14.

Pohl, Robert, "Can the Small Brewer Compete?," in *Brewers Digest*, January 1983, pp. 16–18.

Index

A NOTE ABOUT THE AUTHOR

William Mares is the author of several books. A graduate of Harvard College and the Fletcher School of Law and Diplomacy, he is a schoolteacher and free-lance writer who has contributed to the *Christian Science Monitor, The Economist,* and the Chicago *Sun-Times,* among other publications. He also served in the Vermont state legislature for several terms. Mr. Mares has been a home brewer for more than twenty years.

A NOTE ON THE TYPE

The text of this book was filmset in Aster, a typeface designed by Francesco Simoncini (born 1912 in Bologna, Italy) for Ludwig and Mayer, the German type foundry. Starting out with the basic old-face letter forms that can be traced back to Francesco Griffo in 1495, Simoncini emphasized the diagonal stress by the simple device of extending diagonals to the full height of the letter forms and squaring off. By modifying the weights of the individual letters to combat this stress, he has produced a type of rare balance and vigor. Introduced in 1958, Aster has steadily grown in popularity.

Printed and bound by The Haddon Craftsmen,
Scranton, Pennsylvania

Typography and binding design by Virginia Tan